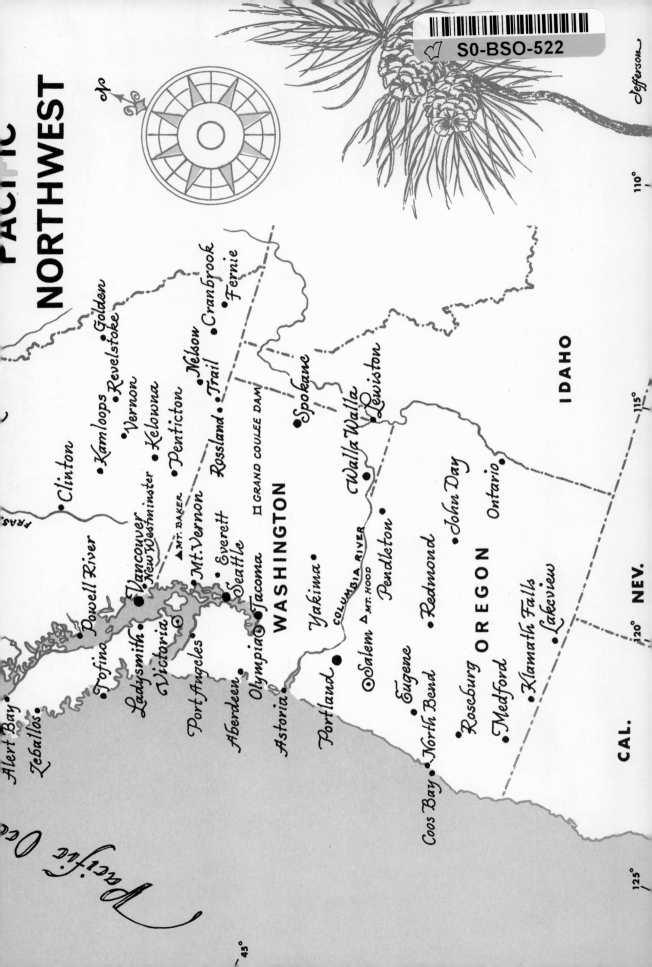

PACIFIC
NORTHWEST

Jefferson

Pacific Oc.

CAL.   NEV.   IDAHO

WASHINGTON

OREGON

Alert Bay
Zeballos
Tofino
Ladysmith
Victoria
Port Angeles
Aberdeen
Olympia
Astoria
Portland
Salem
Eugene
North Bend
Coos Bay
Roseburg
Medford
Klamath Falls
Lakeview

Powell River
Vancouver
New Westminster
Clinton
Kamloops
Revelstoke
Vernon
Kelowna
Penticton
Golden
Melson
Cranbrook
Fernie
Trail
Rossland
GRAND COULEE DAM
MT. BAKER
Mt. Vernon
Everett
Seattle
Tacoma
Yakima
COLUMBIA RIVER
MT. HOOD
Spokane
Walla Walla
Lewiston
Pendleton
Redmond
John Day
Ontario

FRAS.

125°   120°   115°   110°

45°

THE PACIFIC NORTHWEST

Mt. Adams, one of the tallest peaks in the Cascades.

AL MONNER

THE PACIFIC NORTHWEST

STEWART HOLBROOK

NARD JONES

RODERICK HAIG-BROWN

Edited by Anthony Netboy

ILLUSTRATED WITH PHOTOGRAPHS

DOUBLEDAY & COMPANY, INC.

GARDEN CITY, NEW YORK

Contents

Foreword

IF YOU are looking for the road-map and what-to-see kind of guide to the Pacific Northwest, this book is not for you. Such books have value, and there are plenty of them. But this is designed to go deeper than that, to unfold the character as well as the physical appearance of a land rich in natural and human resources.

Three leading writers of the Pacific Northwest have been engaged to interpret that character and articulate it. Each, in keeping with the area's tradition of rugged individualism, has been given liberty to write in his own way. This accounts for a certain diversity of organization. Freedom was felt to be a virtue above uniformity or simplification.

Three-eyed, then—like Vishnu—the book examines the texture of Pacific Northwest civilization, the woodsy tang of its setting, the people and motives that went into its development.

Not everything is seen, of course. There may not be enough about boating if you are a boater, about politics if you are politically minded, about Tacoma if you are a Tacoman. But our authors do supply, we feel, at least a minimum of what should be known about Oregon, Washington, and British Columbia by anyone who lives or visits there. And they do it with indigenous voices that carry the sound and tone of the country as truly as the logger's cry of "tim-burr!"

This is how it looks to those who live in the Pacific Northwest and love it. But they are not uncritical, and their love is born of understanding. Each is an historian, and if the book seems at times too strongly rooted in history, it is because the green leaves of the present and the buds of the future are so dependent upon those roots. As for the personal enthusiasms and dislikes of each writer, we do not expect you to agree with all the conclusions—only to be stimulated into practicing a trait strong among Pacific Northwesterners: that of thinking on your own.

For all its pictorial and segmented content, this book is not primarily one for dipping into; rather, it is for reading through at least a section at a time.

Anyone doing so will acquire a common field of reference which every educated inhabitant of the region is supposed to have.

The picture which emerges is that of a "last frontier" that ignores international boundaries and may be taken generally as a social, economic, and geographic entity. People attracted there seem to share the same penchant for natural beauty, for responding to challenge, for being resourcefully independent and yet conservative in the sense that Thoreau was conservative. They also share related problems. It is our hope that this will prove an indispensable book for newcomers wanting to know and old-timers wishing to be reassured of the heritage and wonders of the Pacific Northwest.

ANTHONY NETBOY

OREGON

Stewart Holbrook

The waves roll in from Cathay on the Oregon coast. Heceta Head lighthouse.

MANY who live in the Pacific Northwest will tell you that it came into being by reason of beaver or gold or an illusion commonly called the Northwest Passage. Any one of the notions will do to explain matters. And so, too, will an even greater simplification:

Much of the entire American West was due to the built-in curiosity of generations of people who merely wanted to see what was on the other side of the mountain. *Any* mountain. Or, for that matter, any river.

Just where the West begins depends a good deal on where you are standing—on where you drove your stakes. Some of us drove ours in Oregon, not far from where the West begins to peter out in tidewater and the waves come rolling in from China.

But I would not dream of telling anybody where the West begins. I am long since housebroken in that regard. It is too delicate and important a subject to be settled by anything short of a national vote. There are even degrees of West among Westerners, although arguments concerning what is basically a matter of geographical status have seldom reached the two-gun stage during recent years. The sneer is more effective, as in the Walla Walla merchant's tone.

"How is everything back here in the East?" he asked as he registered at the Hotel Cheyenne.

To the average Easterner, who has never been there, the Pacific Northwest is a vague and perhaps even mysterious place. He may be familiar with a few striking images—with the Columbia River, with mountains named Hood and Rainier, with Puget Sound and the Olympic Peninsula, and, across the border, with Vancouver Island. Possibly he may recall pictures of skiing, salmon fishing, and a great deal of tall timber. Beyond that, it might almost be terra incognita.

For this and other reasons, the people who live in the Pacific Northwest often complain that they do not get the breaks in what has become known as "vacation literature." Eastern writers and editors seem to believe that our region is still pretty much the province of hunters and trappers, with a few hundred loggers lurking in the woods, trying to let daylight into the forest primeval.

Multnomah Falls, largest in the Pacific Northwest, were discovered in 1792 by Lt. Broughton of Vancouver's expedition on his journey up the Columbia. AL MONNER

This is not strange. Modern history did not begin in our corner of the United States until the cloudy morning of May 11, 1792, when the brig *Columbia,* under Captain Robert Gray, out of Boston, came plunging full sail over a foaming bar that had attracted the skipper's attention while he was cruising along the West Coast looking for furs.

Captain Gray appears to have been the laconic type of Yankee. Three lines in his log serve to bring the ship over the terrible bar and into a stream he judged to be a good ten miles wide near its mouth. Six lines are devoted to bearings and soundings, one line to pumping out the casks and filling them from the stream.

"Then, so ends," he wrote. He might better have written "so begins," for the story of the great river and the Pacific Northwest begins with Captain Gray.

A day or so later, Gray bethought himself to declare this "Columbia's River" and began to trade with the astonished natives, large numbers of whom came out in canoes to the vessel. From among them he got 160 prime sea otter skins, worth up to $100 each in China. Then Gray sailed out of the stream and virtually out of history; but he had discovered, named, and claimed the long-sought "River of the West."

He had espied it and sailed into it in the nick of time, for right behind him was Captain George Vancouver with a British expedition making one final search for the fabled Northwest Passage. Upon learning of Gray's discovery, Vancouver dispatched Lieutenant William R. Broughton to sail across the bar in *H.M.S. Chatham* and then proceed by rowboat upstream for a hundred miles.

Captain Gray had brought genesis to what soon was called simply "The Oregon Country" and is now the states of Oregon, Washington, and Idaho. For purposes of this book, it will be best to begin with Oregon. And, naturally, to understand Oregon, one must know a bit about its past.

In 1803 the United States made the Louisiana Purchase, and soon after came the first official party to explore the vast new region. It was October 1805 when Meriwether Lewis and William Clark first laid eyes on the Columbia, that great surging stream that had been flowing in and out of men's imaginations for many years, and by November 7 they camped where they could see, between the receding banks of the river, the bright expanse of the Pacific. "Ocian in view," Clark wrote in his journal. "O, the joy!"

The expedition's importance in United States history is still in the process of interpretation. Some writers tend to credit it alone for acquisition of the Oregon Country, which was not a part of the Louisiana Purchase and was, at best, of doubtful sovereignty. The late Bernard De Voto believed that the expedition was of paramount importance in regard to Oregon and that its greatest contribution was that it gave the entire West to the American people as "something the mind could deal with."

Before, this void had been a land of rumor, guess, and fantasy. In 1805 Lewis and Clark peopled the unknown with specific tribes of Indians, named its flora and fauna, mapped its mountains, described its varying climates, and dissipated forever the ancient myth of the Northwest Passage. After Lewis and Clark, the mind could focus on reality. And it did: only five years later an American trading post was established near the mouth of the Columbia and a supporting party was making its way overland from St. Louis.

With the purchase of Louisiana began the territorial growth of the United States beyond the Mississippi. Later additions included the annexation of Texas (1845), that of the Oregon Country (1846), and the so-called Mexican Cession (1848). Meanwhile, the Webster-Ashburton Treaty (1842) had seemed to settle the question of the boundary between the United States and Canada. So, periodically, the new trans-Mississippi lands were organized formally into territories, then into states of the union. In the Pacific Northwest, for example, Oregon Territory included what became the states of Oregon, Washington, and Idaho and parts of Montana and Wyoming.

Almost simultaneously, both Britishers and Americans began to converge on Oregon. In the same year that Lewis and Clark came down the Lower Columbia, men of the North West Company of Montreal, fur traders, came over the Canadian Rockies and set about exploring. One of them, David Thompson, who had already found the source of the Columbia, shoved off to follow the stream to its mouth. But when that doughty Briton arrived at what is now Astoria, Oregon, he was dismayed to find a stockaded compound, over which was flying the American flag. The compound was a spearhead of John Jacob Astor's plan to make his American Fur Company into a trading monopoly of North America.

The War of 1812 interfered. In the face of reports that British men-of-war were already in the Pacific, Astor sold Fort Astoria to the North West Company. *H.M.S. Raccoon* entered the Columbia to take possession and, as new Fort George, the post opened for business. At war's end, the Treaty of Ghent declared that all territory, places, and possessions taken by either party from the other should be restored. Fort George was returned to the United States. But Astor decided not to resume operations on the Columbia. The Canadian company was permitted to continue. A convention of joint occupancy was entered into by the two nations.

The Astoria post was soon taken over by the North West Company's ancient competitor, the Hudson's Bay Company, an outfit whose policy in-

The Astor Column at Astoria commemorates founding of the city by John Jacob Astor, and other historical events.

dicated a dogmatic belief in the permanence of the British empire. For more than a century and a half it had seen trading concerns come and go. It was patient with the wisdom of years. It seemed also to be as relentless as time.

The Hudson's Bay Company's governor and gentlemen adventurers were no men to desert the empire in time of need. And so, presently, to Astoria came George Simpson, soon to be knighted, and with him Dr. John McLoughlin, whom Governor Simpson had recently promoted to the post of the Hudson's Bay Company's Chief Factor, to consider matters in this, the new Western Department. At a spot on the Columbia opposite present Portland, they established in 1824 what was to be the company's headquarters in the Oregon Country, with McLoughlin in charge, and christened it Fort Vancouver.

The location of this important post had been chosen with care. It was the natural starting point for parties going south up the Willamette River or overland north to Puget Sound. Although Simpson believed that nothing could stop American settlers from going anywhere they wanted in the Oregon Country, he directed Factor McLoughlin to steer them as far as possible to lands south of the Columbia.

Simpson was right. On came the Yankee settlers—fish packers, fur traders, missionaries, families seeking farms. One and all they came to call on Dr. McLoughlin, who was kind and courteous yet persuasive in urging them to settle south of the Columbia in Oregon's Willamette River Valley. One of the missionaries, the Rev. Jason Lee, opened a Methodist school for Indians in 1835, then turned his talents to politics. Making the rounds of the scattered settlers, almost half of whom were retired veterans of the Bay Company's trap lines, he obtained signatures to a petition asking Congress to provide a territorial status for Oregon, which he sent to Washington. When nothing came of it, Lee left on foot overland for the Atlantic Coast and in person presented a second petition to Congress. Then he went about recruiting more settlers.

In May 1840 Lee returned by ship to the Columbia, bringing with him a party of fifty-one new settlers whom his compelling eloquence had shaken from their native homes. This party went into Oregon history, with capitals, as The Great Enforcement. When later a settler died intestate, the remaining settlers held a meeting with "probate powers." They elected justices of the peace and four constables and named a committee to frame a constitution and draft a legal code. Out of this and other get-togethers came a sort of provisional government that was to last from 1846 until Oregon Territory was formed two years later.

McLoughlin could not contain the Americans south of the Columbia.

Sod house, one of the few still standing, sheltered early settlers in the Steens Mountain country. AL MONNER

They continued to move north, to settle on the Cowlitz River and Puget Sound in present Washington. In 1843 and again in 1845 came really great migrations which, combined, brought some 4000 land-hungry American settlers to rut the Oregon Trail so deep it could be seen a century afterward and to make of the covered wagon a symbol fit to join the *Mayflower* and the cotton gin in the legendry of America.

As long as they lived, the covered-wagon people were to remember the biggest sun and the biggest moon in the biggest skies they had ever seen.

It was the hottest sun, the coldest moon. Mirages danced ahead of their wagons or flickered in their wake, and the youngsters cried with joy, then wept bitterly as a handsome blue lake appeared, shimmering-cool and inviting for a few moments, then sank out of sight into the horizon. It came to seem as if their goal and the horizon were moving in unison and they were not getting anywhere.

The wind on the prairies never ceased. It blew straight out of hell, then from the polar regions. It piled up dark, cloudy murk that split in thunderous crashes, and out of it came salvos of cast-iron hailstones to stun the imagination and fell oxen in their yokes.

The sun was worse than the wind. In the great void of the prairies there was no getting away from the sun. You could not hide from its heat. And just as bad was its confusing brightness. A gopher was seen plainly to be a coyote, a clump of sagebrush became a mounted Indian, and a wrecked and abandoned wagon grew and grew until it loomed up like a monstrous barn, then fused into nothingness.

But on they pushed, and out of the great wagons—when men saw that they must hurry their pace lest they be caught on the trail in a mountain winter—would tumble a massive bureau of carved oak, or a chest, or a chair or two, or even a parlor organ.

Francis Parkman, the historian, saw the furniture strewn along the Oregon Trail. He recognized, as did lesser men, that these things were not the mere trumpery of households; they were the last physical evidences of family status and family continuity. They were not discarded lightly; next to food and powder, they were the last things to be left along the way. A family that jettisoned such articles was a family in desperate straits.

These were among the things talked or thought about in later years when early settlers gathered for reunions and remembered their youths in the circles around campfires that blinked like small red eyes in the endless nights.

By then, these people had long since attained the hallowed status of Pioneers, and they were sure that the Oregon Trail had done something to their character to set them apart from all others in the Oregon Country. Their attitude seemed to be that they had endured the most, hence their needs and opinions should be given first consideration in all regional matters.

I happen to think their attitude was natural, and perhaps it was morally right, too. The Pacific Northwest, and especially that portion of it that became Oregon, was to them more than a territory, more than a state. It was something like hallowed ground. They had cut its first logs. They had cleared and plowed its first fields. They had fought its only war. They had done all this and much more *after* they had already covered the longest wagon trail in history.

You do not perform feats like these and remain without a cult or some special form of aura. Cried one of their number: "Patient toilers of pioneer days, what shall I say of your lonely, isolated lives . . . ?" And she went on to recall the pathetic funerals along the trail and the shuddering apprehension with which the perils of maternity were awaited in dismal wagons or cabins. During an Indian uprising she saw "the slow caravan of returning comrades who bore their mutilated dead." She never forgot "the blinding tears that accompanied the sudden disasters of early times" or "the haunting specter of homesickness that moved about the house and clearing. . . ."

No, you did not emerge unscarred and unchanged from such memories. Man or woman, willing or not, the experience made you over, turned you into the classic character of the Pioneer. The poet Walt Whitman identified these people: they were the ones who had to bear the brunt of danger. It was them upon whom the rest of us depended.

As our pioneers of the Pacific Northwest passed from the flesh, they were immortalized in the arts. The most favored medium was sculpture, and over the years many statues in marble, granite, and bronze have gone up in memory of the men and women of the covered wagons. Wreaths are lavished at their bases, as they are not at the bases of cast-iron generals and politicians.

Occasionally, as in all groups, and especially so with those having to do with pioneers and their descendants, the group becomes a cult and the cultism becomes fatuous. Some sixty years ago, an Oregon pioneer, his nostrils filled with the smoke from remembered campfires and his head empty of generosity for late-comers, stood up at the annual meeting of the Oregon Pioneer Association. "I say to you," he declared, "that there was no honor in having come to a country already opened up."

Many a latter-day immigrant to Oregon has resented this pioneer cultism. I rather enjoy it. Its mild snobbism is harmless. It has its foundations in one of the greatest American experiences. What if it does make for parochialism, as is often charged against Oregonians to the present day? Most of the descendants of pioneers I know do not allow the fact of their antecedents to affect their own decency as human beings. Moreover, the pioneer cult tends to maintain a vicarious pride in one of the classic events in American history. This alone, to my mind, weights the scales in the cult's favor. Anything that makes for pride as an American is good, whether it be a forebear on the *Mayflower*, or one in Bunker's pasture, or one who walked two thousand miles beside a covered wagon.

Yet, more than any other part of the Pacific Northwest, Oregon today is

State capitol at Salem. The pioneer figure on top, looking west, symbolizes westward march of the first white settlers.

believed by non-natives and by many who were born here to be hampered by "old-fashioned attitudes" that permeate the social—and even the business—climate of the region. Critics like to compare the Oregon metropolis of Portland with Seattle to indicate the alleged "backwardness" of the older state as compared to Washington.

As Oregon grew from territory to state, the early settlements fought each other for population with promotional ballyhoo, whispered smear campaigns, and political skulduggery in low and high places. Occasionally an armed mob from one town raided the courthouse of another to steal physical properties of the county seat and remove them to its own struggling metropolis. Indeed, these county-seat wars were so numerous as to become a legend, not only in the Pacific Northwest, but also elsewhere in the West.

Only time could adjust these affairs, and gradually the more fortunate settlements took on the size and importance and flavor for which they were probably destined from the first. Oregon's first permanent white settlement, which had been a trading post, first of John Jacob Astor, then of the Hudson's Bay Company, became Astoria, to survive as a flourishing center of salmon canneries and sawmills.

In the burgeoning period, Oregon City took the lead. Before Portland was little more than a blaze on a fir stump, this town beside the falls of the Willamette had become the biggest and liveliest in all the Pacific Northwest. By 1845, it seemed as if nothing could stop Oregon City. The settlers had formed a Temperance Society, a circulating library with 300 volumes, and the Oregon Falls Lyceum. The *Oregon Spectator* had started publication there. Local Masons had organized the first lodge west of the Missouri River. When the town fathers felt a need for expansion, the new plat was surveyed not with compass and chain but with compass and rope. The rope stretched, then shrank, presenting the town with irregular lots, which it has to this day. The provisional government met there, and for eight years Oregon City was the territorial capital.

Then the later arrivals at new Portland, twelve miles down the Willamette River from Oregon City, began to heed a remark made by Captain John H. Couch.

"To this very point," said he, "to this very point I can bring any ship that can get into the mouth of the Columbia River. And not, sir, a rod farther."

The Portlanders staged a co-operative effort of herculean proportions, laying a thick plank road over the hills to Tualatin Plains, already the center of northern Oregon's great farming country. From this point on, Portland grew while Oregon City faded. When Oregon became a state in 1859, the capital was moved to Salem.

Mining was one of the early attractions in Oregon Territory, but not to the extent it was elsewhere. Western ghost towns have long since become valuable property in former mining states: the veins may have petered out, but not the tourists. Central City, Colorado; Virginia City, Nevada; and Columbia, California, are filled every season with visitors from all over the country. A few of Oregon's old mining camps survive as ghost towns; Jack-

Portland, "City of Roses," with Mt. Hood in the background.   AL MONNER

sonville, in Jackson county, is far and away the best preserved of the lot, thanks to the local Historical Society, whose museum has an outstanding collection of artifacts. The state's gold strikes lay in two widely separated areas—the southwestern diggings in Josephine and Jackson counties, begun in 1851, and the eastern Oregon diggings, located in Grant and Baker counties in 1861. Relics of the eastern mines center around Canyon City, Baker, Sumpter, Bourne, Granite, Auburn, and Homestead.

Then there is, or was, an ugly blot on the map called Copperfield.

Jacksonville in Jackson County is the best preserved of Oregon's ghost mining towns.

Copperfield no longer exists. The site is historic because it was the scene of one of Oregon's most dramatic and amusing events. In 1913, after Copperfield had established a scandalous reputation as a hard-drinking, wide-open mining town, Governor Oswald West sent his private secretary, Miss Fern Hobbs, armed with authority and a small detachment of the National Guard, to close Copperfield's illegal saloons and honky-tonks and declare a state of martial law. This "Toughest Town in the State" never recovered from the ignominy of successful regulation by the spunky Miss Hobbs, who weighed 104 pounds fully dressed, and she promptly became a sensation on the front pages of newspapers the country over. In Oregon a group of militant suffragettes rose up and started a "Fern Hobbs for Governor" boom. But Miss Hobbs was no feminist.

Obtaining equal rights for women in the Pacific Northwest had long been the consuming ambition of Oregon's Abigail Scott Duniway. Idaho and Washington had granted the vote before Oregon fell into line in 1912, a year before Miss Hobbs cowed Copperfield.

This time lag seems odd in view of the fact that, as early as 1902, Oregon passed a constitutional amendment providing for the initiative, the referendum, and the recall and also for a presidential primary and state-printed textbooks for the schools. These laws, called The Oregon System, were the first of their kind in the United States and were generally credited to the efforts of William S. U'Ren, a Portland attorney and single taxer. But then Oregon has periodically been no model of constancy. In 1931, for example, soon after the state had elected many officials who campaigned openly as members of the Ku-Klux Klan, it elected a Jew, Julius L. Meier, as Governor. What's more, Meier turned out to be a better than average chief executive.

Oregon has kept well abreast of her sister states in legislative enactments and constitutional amendments.

The Australian ballot was introduced in 1901, and U'Ren's intensive campaign resulted in adoption of the initiative and referendum in 1902, the direct primary in 1904, and the recall in 1908. Oregon adopted workmen's compensation and widows' pensions in 1913, compulsory education in 1912, and a system of public-utility districts to generate and sell electric power in 1930. Being less socialistically minded than Washington, Oregon has not pushed the PUD movement as far. The recall has been used to get rid of politicians who are ineffectual in office, such as Sheriff "Mike" Elliott of Portland some years ago, and occasionally to remove troublesome school-board members.

On the whole, Oregon has been in the van of legislative progress in this country. It passed a Fair Employment Act as far back as 1949. Yet it remains a conservative state. Historians are fond of pointing out that the state was solidly Republican for over four decades of this century, then in the mid-1950s switched to the Democrats even while a Republican sat in the White House. Students of our political history were not surprised when the tide turned again and we elected a Republican governor in 1958, though we still had two Democratic senators—one the maverick Wayne Morse—and three out of four Democratic representatives.

Patriotism in the state is well subdued. Nonetheless, Oregonians were among the first American troops in overseas service during World War I and showed their mettle in the famous battles of Château-Thierry and Belleau Wood. In the Second World War we had 148,000 men in service, of whom 2835 were killed. On the night of June 21, 1942, history was made when a Japanese submarine shelled Fort Stevens on the coast near the mouth of the Columbia. This was the only actual shelling of the United States mainland during the war. No casualties or damages were caused by the erratic marksmanship.

The war changed Oregon considerably. Thousands of persons who had only a dim idea of what the state was like came to Portland to work in the shipyards, and jerry-built towns sprang up to house these well-paid migrants. One was Vanport, destined to be wiped out during the 1948 flood on the Columbia River. Aluminum mills were built at Troutdale, as well as at Vancouver and at Longview, Washington. Thus heavy industry, lacking before, made its appearance and started a clamor for industrialization that has never let up. The population of the state jumped to 1,500,000 by 1950, giving some of us the feeling that we were becoming crowded, even though our population density per square mile is slight—less than a quarter of California's and about one-sixteenth of New York's. In the 1950s the population influx slackened considerably, and in the next ten years only 250,000 people were added.

We have not been able to attract much industry since World War II, for reasons that are none too clear. Some say it's the rainy climate, others the cool attitude of many natives who hate belching smokestacks. Perhaps the real reason is a certain lack of enterprise.

State officials are proud of the recent creation of the Boardman Space Age Industrial Park in the eastern Oregon desert, on which the Boeing Company has taken a lease. Scientists tell us that the area around Bend, which is not in the Industrial Park, more closely resembles the surface of the moon than any other spot in North America, a bit of news which has intrigued the promoters of industry. But Oregon is almost at the bottom of the list among states in defense contracting and thus is happily still free of the clutter of military installations and defense industries that have defaced much of the landscape in neighboring states.

The state celebrated its centennial in 1959 with a fair and exposition that failed to impress many out-of-staters who came here. Lacking the brash boosterism of Seattle's Century 21 hoopla, the centennial was promoted in a low key: the exhibits were generally less than spectacular and the celebrations largely centered around the cult of the pioneer. Significantly, Oregon's centennial was a tribute to the past while Seattle's wingding celebrated the future.

Downtown Portland. Snow-rain is common in Oregon in winter.　　　AL MONNER

If Oregon has settled down in the second half of the twentieth century to the workaday business of expanding its industry and agriculture, its trade with the rest of the nation and the world, and becoming one of the great tourist attractions of the West, it still does not live by bread alone. Attention to the refinements of life has attracted or bred such creative talents as Ernest Bloch in music, Pietro Belluschi in architecture, and Carl Morris among artists. The Oregon Shakespearean Festival at Ashland has long been a cultural event of more than regional significance.

The cultural sap has perhaps run strongest in the literary field. Since Oregon is a state that has become noted for the diversity and independence of its creative artists' views, it will startle no one to recall that iconoclast John Reed was a Portland boy before he saw the Bolshevik triumph while standing beside Lenin and Trotsky, wrote *Ten Days that Shook the World*, and was buried in the Kremlin. Some other Oregon writers of national repute are Charles Erskine Scott Wood, onetime grand old man of Oregon letters; James Stevens, a sawmill worker at Bend whom H. L. Mencken encouraged to write *Paul Bunyan*, which became a whopping success and touched off a Bunyan craze that continues to smolder today; Ernest Haycox, prolific author of Western stories; H. L. Davis, whose *Honey in the Horn* won the Pulitzer Prize for fiction; and Nancy Wilson Ross, among others.

Any brief survey of Oregon is bound to paddle for a time along the Columbia River.

One of the river's first publicists was William Cullen Bryant, a young Yankee poet who wrote about "the continuous woods where rolls the Oregon, and hears no sound save his own dashings." He had never been within 3000 miles of the majestic stream about which he wrote, and he seems not to have known it had already been named the Columbia. This ignorance of the enormous country drained by the river is typical of that which so widely prevails today. Yet the thought of the great lonely stream moved young Bryant powerfully. He was right, too, in making it the first symbol of the Oregon Country.

Oregon's traditional disunion has rarely included opposition to efforts to discipline the vagaries of the Columbia River. Here in the big stream was something to unify the thinking of all who lived along its banks. British Columbia, Washington, and Oregon—each wanted this or that done to control the river's flow. The covered-wagon pioneers never forgot the tragedies due to the river's wild dashings or the heartbreaking labor of the portages around the falls of Celilo and the Cascades. Those who came by sea were immediately harassed by the dangerous bar at the river's mouth and by the treacherous channel after they entered the stream. Once farms and towns had been created, the river had a way of suddenly rising—as in 1894—above the highest visible or known watermark, all the way from its headwaters to Portland, and washing buildings, animals, and crops, sometimes entire towns, down to the sea. The 1948 flood was almost as disastrous.

Farther up, in the long stretches between Walulla and Canada, and somewhat later in time, came the wheat ranchers, who at first marveled that they could plow and sow the bunch-grass lands and raise fifty bushels to the acre and within a few years discovered that the moisture in the soil had been exhausted and ten bushels was an average crop. Nothing but water would alleviate this condition, and the only water nearby was that of the Columbia, flowing past the powdery acres at the bottom of a canyon from 300 to 500 feet deep. Most of the wheat men must have dreamed of getting water somehow; yet, for a long time, irrigation was only a dream, and many went away.

Then there were imaginative men who looked at the surging power that came hurrying in such volume from the snows and glaciers of a vast region which included the high backbone of the continent and wondered how this immensity could be dammed and made to turn turbines. These were bold men who thought of damming, for the Columbia is an arrogant piece of water. There is nothing yielding about it, nothing submissive, nothing that could be called considerate.

For all this dreaming about flood control and irrigation and power and navigation canals, the first improvements on the river were little portage tramways at the falls of Celilo and the Cascades. These became steam railways and continued to operate until the flood of 1894, when the line at the Cascades was destroyed. Early petitions to Congress had demanded that locks be constructed at the Cascades. Twenty years later, in 1896, the Cascade Locks were declared ready. Their busiest year was 1905, when 1417 boats went up or down. By then, demands in Congress were for a canal and locks at Celilo.

The engineers moved to the grimly dramatic ledges and boulders above The Dalles in Oregon, where the river boiled and roared for more than ten miles, and for twelve years they blasted and drilled a path around the rapids. Opened in 1915, the eight-mile canal had competition not only from the railroads but from a paved highway along the Columbia. By 1920, the canal and locks at Celilo lay virtually idle. One by one, the stern-wheelers on the river were retired, but wheat and other traffic revived when steel barges pulled by tugboats were introduced.

The Celilo Canal and the North Jetty at the river's mouth were the last major improvements by government agencies on the Columbia in two dec-

Grain elevators dot the landscape around Pendleton.

ades, or until completion of Bonneville Dam in 1938. Bonneville, however, was not the first dam across the Columbia. That distinction belongs to the Rock Island Dam below Wenatchee, built by the Puget Sound Power and Light Company and finished in 1931. This project and Bonneville ushered in what the people of the Pacific Northwest think of as "The Dam Era" on the Columbia.

By the time Rock Island was producing power, the United States Corps of Engineers was under way with an over-all survey of American rivers,

Bonneville was the first federal multipurpose dam on the Columbia.

including the Columbia. The survey held that dams should be built not for navigation alone but for "multiple purposes." Dams were to help maintain an even flow throughout the year. They would permit slack-water navigation for long stretches. They should supply water for irrigation, and they should generate electricity.

Work was begun in 1933 on a dam named for Captain Benjamine Louis Eulalie de Bonneville, French-born graduate of West Point, whose career has long been a matter of some controversy but which, in any case, made him a prominent figure in the old Oregon Country through his dabbling

Curling fish ladders help adult salmon get over Bonneville Dam.

in the fur trade and, later, by reason of his being the first commandant at Vancouver Barracks in Washington Territory. Bonneville Dam was built just below the falls of the Cascades, around which the canal and locks had been completed in 1896.

At last the "Great Shute," as Lewis and Clark called it—the place of labored portage for trappers, immigrants, steamboat freight and passengers—lay untroubled in the quiet waters behind Bonneville Dam. The dreaded barrier was gone. The lock was opened to pass the *Charles L. Wheeler,* which proceeded upriver to be the first deep-sea vessel to dock at The Dalles and to make that rapids-fenced city, 44 miles above Bonneville, a port of the Pacific Ocean. Transmission of power from the Bonneville turbines started in 1938.

Not only the Great Shute disappeared in the impounded waters. With it went the physical evidences of the Bridge of the Gods, which most condescending white people referred to as "a favorite myth" of the Indians. This was a natural stone arch under which, so the natives told the pioneers, the canoes of their ancestors had floated in the days before the various gods who inhabited the Cascade Mountains had begun to war among themselves and started throwing smoke, fire, and boulders, with the result that the bridge collapsed and forced the river into a new channel.

Possibly the greatest interest shown by the public in Bonneville centers on the arrangements provided for the migration of salmon. There are three fishways, one at each end of the spillway dam and one across the face of the powerhouse. Each consists of a collection system and a fish ladder, with a pair of fish locks on both shores. Each ladder is an inclined flume, forty feet wide, in which is installed a series of fish weirs. The weirs create successive pools, each a foot higher than the next one downstream. The ladders circle around the ends of the dam and powerhouse, permitting adult fish heading upstream to reach the higher water above the dam. The volume of water flowing down the ladder is regulated to induce the fish to swim rather than leap from one pool to another.

It is the fish-counting stations that attract most visitors to Bonneville Dam. Near the head of each ladder is a small house beside a pool, in which there is a picketed barrier with three openings. The counter in the little house can open any or all of the gates. The floor of each gate is painted white in order to light the forms of the fish as they pass quickly across it. This makes identification by species easy for the trained personnel in the counting stations. It also does a great deal more: it gives visitors the feeling of participation, even if only as watchers, in the incomparable mystery of salmon migrations. There they see for a brief moment big fish and medium fish moving across the patch of white paint, returning from their long sojourn at sea to home waters for procreation and death.

Many visitors want to know about the different species of salmon counted and even the different kinds of fish. Over a ten-year period, the average annual count included 359,054 Chinooks, 127,431 steelhead trout, 72,834 bluebacks, 9437 silvers, 1600 chums, 22,426 shad, 13,458 carp, 132,730 suckers, 59,750 squawfish, plus miscellaneous bullheads, crappies, bass, and sturgeon. There was also an average of 105,128 lamprey eels counted every year.

The downstream-migrating fingerlings go over the spillways or pass

Over this flashboard at Bonneville Dam some 800,000 fish—mostly Chinook, steelhead and blueback salmon—are counted annually.

through the turbines or are conducted through four bypasses provided with entrances at points where fish are most apt to arrive at the dam.

After the fish going upriver have passed Bonneville, they climb similar ladders on the Columbia at The Dalles Dam, McNary, and Rock Island: they come to the end of the line at the Chief Joseph Dam, which has no passage. In a few years they will also have to pass John Day Dam, now under construction between Bonneville and McNary. The main runs of steelhead and spring Chinook leave the Columbia to go up the Snake, where the fish must scale Ice Harbor, Ox Bow, and Brownlee dams.

The story of the Pacific salmon is dramatic and also melancholy. When Lewis and Clark came into the Oregon Country, nearly every river and stream that flowed into the Snake and Columbia and every coastal stream from British Columbia down to Monterey teemed with salmon and/or steelhead. The Columbia River Indians worshiped the salmon and honored him with magical rites because he was the staple of their diet, along with roots and berries. But in the later nineteenth century the white man, seeking profits, brought his seines and traps and fish wheels into nearly every cove and headland. Salmon was packed and sent to eastern markets and later to London, Paris, Valparaiso, and even the Orient, where the red-flaked fish brought high prices. Fish canning became big business, and by 1880 there were about 40 canneries on the Columbia River in Oregon, from Astoria to Celilo Falls. But this prosperity subsided by the turn of the century and the overfished stocks simply would not yield enough fish to keep all the canners in business.

Advent of the power dams on the Columbia and some of its tributaries dealt another blow to the salmon: many streams became impassable because of dams built with inadequate fishways; others were clogged with the slash and debris of logging operations; or were dried up in summer by irrigation withdrawals. Paper mills added their slime and communities their sewage to the rivers, choking the fish. Indians, who had almost unrestricted fishing rights wherever they lived and were uncanny netters and spearers, took a heavy toll of the breeding stocks of Columbia River salmon.

State and federal governments have spent large sums on improving spawning grounds, building fish ladders and other devices at dams, operating hatcheries to build up the stocks, and investigating every conceivable aspect of the life of the salmon. They are even experimenting with electronic guides to shoo the fingerlings and adults around the big dams. But the runs of Chinook and steelhead are declining; sports and commercial fishermen fight about fishing seasons, gear, and "bag" limits in a way that sometimes threatens civil war. All but one of Oregon's coastal streams has been closed to commercial fishing. Canned tuna is replacing salmon as a favorite on the market, and it is claimed that local canneries are forced to go as far afield as Africa for tuna. All of which indicates choppy waters ahead for the fishing industry in Oregon.

The story of Grand Coulee and of other dams below it will be found elsewhere in this book. Bonneville is significant not only because it was the first government-built dam on the main Columbia but also because it was the first project resulting from the so-called Review Report of the Corps of Engineers, a document which, as implemented in the last twenty years, has changed the river almost beyond knowing. If all the recommenda-

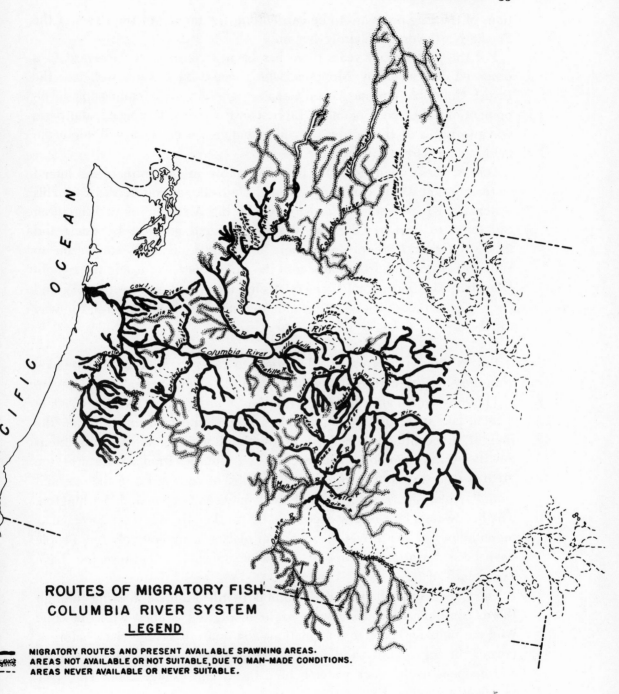

ROUTES OF MIGRATORY FISH
COLUMBIA RIVER SYSTEM
LEGEND

MIGRATORY ROUTES AND PRESENT AVAILABLE SPAWNING AREAS.
AREAS NOT AVAILABLE OR NOT SUITABLE, DUE TO MAN-MADE CONDITIONS.
AREAS NEVER AVAILABLE OR NEVER SUITABLE.

The salmon's migratory routes have been severely curtailed by dams, pollution, blockades, and irrigation withdrawals.

tions of the Engineers are to be carried out, the taming of the rivers of the Pacific Northwest has hardly begun.

For the past several years there has been a controversy in regard to a proposed dam at Libby, Montana, which would back water well into the British Columbia interior. When Canada signs the treaty calling for development of the Upper Columbia, Libby construction will proceed, and dams will rise north of the border. In any event, more changes will surely be made in the Great River of the West.

One of these changes could be conceivably in the form of an inland waterway that would connect the Columbia to Puget Sound. Plans for this waterway, which would be constructed by the Army Corps of Engineers, call for it to start at Olympia, Washington, and go west by dams and locks to Grays Harbor. From there a dredged channel would run to Willapa Harbor and, from there, into the Columbia River inside the treacherous bar. The benefits to commercial shipping would be considerable, and Oregon powerboat men would be able to cruise by inland route all the way to Alaska.

Let us move now from the historical to the geographical and quickly scan the physical features, the wildlife, and the natural resources of Oregon.

The state's main artery is, of course, the Columbia River, which begins in a small lake in British Columbia that lies blue and cold and high on the roof of the continent, hemmed in by the Rockies and the tumultuous Selkirks. From Columbia Lake, swelled by tributaries from seven states, the great stream surges its tortured way a matter of 1200 miles to the sea, and from Pasco to Astoria it forms the border between Oregon and Washington. The headwaters lake is now accessible by car, but though it's a spectacular mountainous drama of water, stone, and glacier, comparatively few people have been there. I can't understand why, unless it is because few have ever heard of its glories.

The Canadian portion of the Columbia is still primitive, flowing through those "continuous woods" Bryant wrote about, and is filled with the same wild dashings he heard in imagination—465 miles of savage river before it crosses the forty-ninth parallel to enter the United States, where it slows and deepens in the slack water behind the Grand Coulee Dam. The river has been tamed.

The Columbia is the only stream that managed to hammer its way through the Cascade Mountains. Nowhere else in this immense range is there a passage. Through it went the covered wagons of the Oregon Trail. More importantly, the Cascades split the Northwest into two widely contrasting climates. The slowly moving pioneers could hardly fail to notice it.

For a thousand miles they had passed through a region of light rainfall and sparse vegetation. The winter was cold, the summer blistering. But as they came down the Columbia through these mountains, by boat or by a trail along the river's south bank, the sagebrush changed to tall trees of gigantic girth, the sky turned to lead, mist swirled around the headlands, and gentle rains began to fall. They passed beyond the common range of magpies and rattlesnakes, beyond the fields of powdered lava, out of the land of terrible distances, and entered the largest forest of big trees in America.

The contrast remains. The Cascades in Oregon divide two climates, the effects of which can be seen, heard, and felt. Between residents of the two sides there has developed a subtle difference in speech and even more difference in the shade and depth of their skin tans from sun and wind. The Cascades often divide political thought in Oregon as well.

Eastern Oregon is a land of particular contrasts and complexities. In it are the well-publicized Wallowa Mountains, along with lava beds of an immensity to make one reflect on the convulsions of nature that bred them. And there is the High Desert, a haunted country with the loneliness of infinite distances, of endless rimrock marked with solitary buttes that are coal-black one moment, purple the next. It is also a land where ever-present winds make melancholy music on the lutes formed by telephone wires.

Bordering the desert is the Malheur Wildlife Refuge, some 200,000 acres of marsh, hills, rock, semiarid plains, ponds, rivers, and lakes, to which come millions of birds. Among these feathered boarders who know a good thing are pelicans, cranes, swans, egrets, terns, avocets, killdeers, and numerous songbirds. Here they rest and rear their young before flapping off in great flocks to their other homes.

Also bordering the eastern Oregon desert, in an astonishing pattern, are the park-like ponderosa pine forests, which range north in a vast green carpet through eastern Washington and account in large part for the industrial income of the area.

Once the Cascades are crossed, the influence of the Japanese Current, a sort of Pacific Gulf Stream, is apparent. Western Oregon and Washington are often called "The Evergreen Land." This is no fancy concocted by chambers of commerce. It *is* green from January through December. Rain makes it so, and rain falls to the amount of 130 inches annually in parts of the coastal strip, while inland to the top of the Cascades it varies from some 40 inches in the valleys to 80 inches at higher elevations.

The greatest single natural feature of Western Oregon is the Douglas fir forest. It reaches from the California border up through Oregon, Washington, and British Columbia into Alaska. From it, comes a considerable portion of every earned dollar that circulates in Oregon.

Douglas fir, America's prime timber tree, is cut in patches; it reseeds naturally from the sides. OREGON FORESTRY DEPT.

A great deal of this virgin timber stands in several national forests and two national parks, Rainier and Olympic. "Civilized" logging operators, now working on the proposition that timber is a crop, no longer leave cutover acres to the vagaries of fire and disease but guard their second growth, as they would a treasure, in enormous tree farms.

These vast forests harbor a variety of small and big game. East of the Cascades roam the Rocky Mountain elk, mule deer, and fleet-footed prong-horned antelope, while west of the Cascades hunters prey upon the black-tailed deer and occasionally on the white-tailed deer and Roosevelt elk.

Crater Lake, remnant of a volcano's casing, is dyed by minerals and light an intense blue, unmatchable anywhere.   ANSEL ADAMS

The great Tillamook Fire devastated 325,000 acres of Douglas fir and associated species.

AL MONNER

The wreck of the Peter Iredale *at Hammond Beach near Astoria.*

In the craggy peaks of the Wallowas you may see mountain goats, and in the Hart Mountains of Lake County are some California bighorn sheep.

The Oregon Game Commission says that deer and possibly elk are more numerous today than when the pioneers broke into the Oregon Country. In some places they are eating farmers out of their crops and decimating forest plantations. At any rate, more deer are killed in Oregon by licensed hunters than in any other state of the union—some 146,000 in 1959. In that year, 9000 elk were slaughtered, mostly by city-bred nimrods. Many of the deer are shot with bows and arrows.

Although civilization has substantially reduced their numbers, Oregon harbors a variety of upland game birds, particularly pheasants, grouse, and quail, with some partridge. Ducks and geese come by the millions, and hunters usually take their quotas without much trouble. In 1959 they shot more than 375,000 pheasants, 225,000 quail, and 53,000 partridges.

Even the fur trapper is still found in our state, as in the days of the Hudson's Bay Company. From the Game Commission's reports you learn that licensed trappers take about 25,000 beavers and 34,000 muskrats annually. In the coastal counties mink is bred for its valuable pelt, and the associated fur farmers have organized a co-operative fishing fleet which sails the high seas and brings back fish that are ground into a meal that is the protein staple of the mink's diet. Low market values, says the Game Commission, offer little incentive for trapping the badger, raccoon, bobcat, fox, and coyote, so some of these are slaughtered under the bounty system.

The many streams that tumble down the western slopes of the Cascades into the Columbia and Willamette, or directly into the ocean, are well stocked with steelhead, salmon, and trout, although, as we have seen, refuse from the paper mills and sewage from river towns are greatly reducing the abundance of fish.

One of Oregon's greatest sights is Crater Lake. It is just that—a lake in the remnant of a volcano's casing. But what a lake! Until I saw it, I thought the intense blue reflected from souvenir post cards and Kodachrome photos was the work of a master in the mixing of colored inks. But it is really there, due to minerals and light. It is unlikely that there is a blue to match it anywhere.

Equally as striking as this inland water wonder are the scenes along the Oregon coast, where hunching cliffs and mighty rocks stand against the many moods of the sea. Some of those moods are furious, and remnants of many wrecked ships litter the iridescent beaches.

The greatest man-made sight in our state is a shameful scar in western Oregon, the Tillamook Burn—some 325,000 acres of devastated virgin timber. This is a reminder of what may well have been the most extensive forest fire of all time. Those of us who saw it burn will never forget watching 500 years of forest growth destroyed in ten days of hellish flames. It is unfortunate that conventional Oregon boosters do not make the Big Burn a tourist attraction. As a warning, it surely has more power than volumes of dismal statistics. Besides, near the tragic reminder are some 200,000 acres of the Clatsop Tree Farm, a sample of the many more such privately owned and operated reservoirs of forestation in the Northwest.

The largest—in fact, the only large—city in Oregon is Portland. To help you understand its character, I'll say that, as between Oregon and Washington, I'd as soon live in one state as the other, but in the matter of Portland and Seattle, I prefer Portland. I have lived in both cities and find Portland more comfortable, possibly because I think of it as an overgrown country town. It still retains some of its village charm.

Seattle's character is simple and crystal-clear. It is the perennial boomtown, gay and grim by turns, but always loud and lively, brassy and friendly, a blackslapping place given to roaring, bragging vision. Indeed, it is just the sort of city that would *want* to stage a World's Fair. I can think of nothing more typical than that Seattle's tallest building should bear a legend calling attention to its eminence: here stands *the 42-story* L. C. Smith building.

The Pacific Northwest's second most populous city, Portland, with about 400,000 inhabitants, is a deep-sea port more than 100 miles from the Pacific. Though less spectacular than Seattle's, its setting is dramatic enough, what with two major rivers flowing past or through the town and two major snow-capped peaks—Mt. Hood and Mt. St. Helens—rising from the somberly beautiful Cascades in the background.

The older part of the city spreads west from the Willamette River, then mounts to the semicircle of modest hills called The Heights. The city's east side is flanked by both the Willamette and the Columbia. Our French-looking Willamette and the perverse way we pronounce it, with the accent on the second syllable, is due to the many workings-over it has suffered during the past century. It is of Indian origin and may formerly have been "Wahlmet."

One of the oldest cities in all the American West, Portland was settled in some part by conservatively energetic Yankees, whose magnificent heritage is to be seen in the many acres of elm-shaded village greens which form a sort of Boston Common, called The Park Blocks, almost inviolate these past hundred years. The pioneer Yankees also bequeathed attitudes and institutions, which took such forms as a magnificent public library, an outstanding liberal arts college called Reed, a well-endowed art museum, and three other centers of learning—Portland State College, the University of Portland, and Lewis and Clark College. Add, too, the oldest and largest bookstore in the Pacific Northwest and a newspaper, *The Oregonian*, that observed its one hundredth year in 1950.

For these and other reasons, including an almost continuous series of lectures, debates, and dramatic productions in the Newmarket Theater, built in 1875 at a cost of $100,000, it was not astonishing that a visitor from the Atlantic Coast remarked as early as the late 1870s that Portland, Oregon, was then truly "the Athens of the West."

It is nice, of course, to live in the Athens of the West (do I hear the

The Willamette River separates the west and east sides of Portland.   AL MONNER

disputatious cries of San Franciscans?), but a really great disservice was done to Portland by its founding fathers. These were two Yankee immigrants, Asa L. Lovejoy from Massachusetts and Francis Pettygrove from Maine. For twenty-five cents Lovejoy acquired a half interest in a site on the west bank of the Willamette River. This investment paid for the filing fee. His partner, Pettygrove, had to pay fifty dollars in store goods for his half.

These two optimists felled a few trees of the thick forest of Douglas fir that covered the site, platted four streets, and then paused to consider

Newmarket Theater, most elegant in Pacific Northwest when it opened in 1875, has recently served as a garage, is now a warehouse. AL MONNER

a name for the future metropolis. Pettygrove won the toss of a coin and chauvinistically called the place "Portland" for the principal city of his native Maine, thus perpetrating the most notable opportunity in the United States for the misdirection of mail. But it could have been worse. Lovejoy, who possessed no more of a soaring imagination than his partner, had been set on calling it "Boston."

It is clear that these two men, for all their pioneering ability, had little feeling for the poetry of names. They had it in their power to make Oregon's future metropolis a musical Willamette or a distinctive Multnomah. But

Portland it became, in 1845, and four years later an all-wise U. S. Post Office Department approved the choice with an office and a big round postmark. Portland, Oregon, has borne this major handicap along with twenty-two other Portlands in America and one Portland Junction. Several years ago a committee among us who believed it a burden worth eliminating staged a brief but spirited campaign to change it to Multnomah, the name of the county to which Portlanders pay their real-estate taxes. Though the effort brought many letters favoring the change, we got nowhere with it.

As the urban center of the Beaver State, Portland is an observer and preserver of many fine traditions. One of these is enshrined in a landmark that many visitors to the city miss, perhaps because it dates from the Lewis and Clark Exposition of 1905 and is considered by some residents to be "old hat." Locally it is known as "the biggest log cabin on Earth": it was built entirely of logs with the bark on. Its lofty interior can be described as awesome, and rightly so. More properly it is called the Forestry Building, and it stands as a period piece beyond compare, a monument to Oregon's number-one position as a United States timber reserve and to the state's billion-dollar forest products industry.

Another Oregon tradition is the growing of roses, said to be "second nature" for Oregonians. Portland is the "Rose City." Its week-long Rose Festival in June attracts the largest crowds of visitors to the state. To be elected Festival Rose Queen is the greatest honor a young woman can have, and she and her princesses are attended by the Royal Rosarians during the event. In Portland, too, are the International Rose Test Gardens, whose officials comprise a sort of authority on the admission of new varieties. Even the Pendleton Roundup, the famed annual "Western" event staged in the small city of that name in eastern Oregon, is of secondary importance to the celebration of Oregon's roses.

Since World War II, Oregon has changed in many ways and Portland has lost much of its leisurely, idyllic, unspoiled nineteenth-century air. Stately Victorian mansions like the Corbett home, the Kamm house, and the Portland Hotel have vanished, to be replaced by parking lots and bus stations. A large chunk of old Portland along the Willamette River has been razed in the name of urban renewal. The frame houses and shady lawns will be replaced some day, we are told, by commercial buildings, factories, and motels. Right now the area resembles the aftermath of an aerial bombardment. Well-dressed scavengers can be seen among the rubble, picking up bricks for their patios and digging up plants for their yards.

Portland's commissioners have approved construction of the Foothills Freeway in the heart of the city. This project, financed with 92 per cent federal highway funds, will take some $20,000,000 worth of property off the

Interior of Forestry Building in Portland, built for Lewis and Clark Exposition of 1905. PORTLAND CHAMBER OF COMMERCE

Hood River Valley, in the shadow of Mt. Hood, grows fine apples and other fruit.
AL MONNER

tax rolls, including many splendid churches and synagogues and little wooden houses with quaint porches and gingerbread overhangs. Those of us who protested the freeway were drowned out by the clamor of businessmen shouting that we were impeding progress. The net gain of the freeway will be that motorists will save two or three minutes getting through the city.

It is a long drop in population from Portland to Oregon's other cities, such as Salem, Eugene, Medford, and Corvallis, the biggest of which is only about one-ninth Portland's size.

Most of these other cities are noted as centers for lumber mills or as farm marketing areas. Salem, besides being the state capital, is a fruit and berry hub whose local boosters are known as the Cherrians. For many years, too, Salem was noted for its flax, when the manufacture of linen was the chief industry at the Oregon Penitentiary. Medford is a complex of sawmills and orchards; of late years, it has come to be identified mostly with fine pears. Eugene and Corvallis are noted as the sites of the University of Oregon and Oregon State University, respectively. Astoria is the center of the salmon-fishing industry.

All sorts of agricultural products are grown in Oregon, whose farms and ranches yield about $450,000,000 a year. Tillamook, for instance, is noted for its cheese, which is shipped the world over. To Oregonians, the Hood River Valley means fine apples. The Willamette Valley has the largest areas in cropland and is certainly one of America's most fertile farm areas: it is said to be capable of feeding 12,000,000 people. Strawberries, walnuts, filberts, and prunes are grown almost everywhere in this wide, long valley, all the way from the Columbia to Eugene. And so is holly. Here rain is plentiful from October through May, though in summer the farmers have to haul out their sprinkling pipes.

In eastern Oregon irrigation and dry-land farming are the rule. The farms are no longer farms but huge wheat ranches wherever ten or more inches of rain fall from October to June. Some of the land is cultivated and left fallow every other year to give the soil a chance to store up moisture and nitrogen. On the irrigated lands, as in the Snake River Valley, water is tapped from the river to grow specialty crops of high value, such as potatoes, of which all Oregonians are proud; sugar beets, processed right where they grow; hops; truck crops; and even watermelons, which tourists eat juicily as they ride across the warm, dry country in summer.

But it is really cattle and sheep that characterize business in eastern Oregon. Some of the cattle ranches run to hundreds of thousands of acres operated by cattle kings who live in palatial air-conditioned ranch houses, drive Cadillacs to town, go to Palm Springs for the winter, and live in ducal splendor on their sagebrush lands. Some of these men came to Oregon in the Second Migration—during the 1930s—when Oklahomans deserted their Dust Bowl, bought land cheap, and garnered permits to run cattle on government land. Today they reap the opulent harvest of their labors. With the federal government owning much of the forest and grazing land in the state, these ranchers run their cattle and sheep in the higher, mountainous national forests or Bureau of Land Management holdings in summer and on the lower ranges, mostly privately owned, in the spring and fall. Most of these outfits have enough farmland to grow the hay and grain needed for carrying their cattle and sheep through the winter.

Cattle are moved in the spring from the high mountain country to lower grazing lands.
AL MONNER

Cattle ranches abound in central Oregon, yet a single vast sawmill in Bend annually cuts 200,000,000 board feet of ponderosa lumber from the neighboring forest. The city of Burns, in eastern Oregon, was formerly the capital of the old-time cattle empire; it still has the flavor of a range town, yet almost in the suburbs is a lumber plant with an annual output in excess of 100,000,000 board feet.

And thus, though livestock and agriculture loom large in Oregon's economy and there has also been a lot of talk about the recent diversifica-

Oregon lumber is shipped around the world.

tion of industry, there can be no question as to the first business in Oregon: it is wood products, including pulp, paper, plywood, particle board, and hardboard.

Even in Eugene, seat of the University of Oregon, forest products are the chief industry. This is also true of the Klamath Falls region, where sheep, cattle, and potatoes are secondary to 350,000,000 board feet of lumber cut annually in local mills. Much of southwestern Oregon is now dominated by the sawmills and plywood factories centering on Coos Bay. In this region

Logging in Mt. Hood National Forest.

AL MONNER

are major stands of Port Orford (white) cedar, which is virtually impervious to wood-eating insects. A minor industry here is the working of myrtle wood into souvenirs for tourists.

In theory, for every acre of forest that goes through the sawmills and manufacturing plants, an acre of wilderness—the delight of nature lovers—must be sacrificed. But the situation is not nearly so simple. What for centuries was the lumber industry is today something vastly different. It is properly described as the forest-products industry.

The change first became dramatically apparent with the disappearance of the old-time refuse burner. Twenty-five years ago this piece of equipment was an integral part of every sawmill in the Pacific Northwest. It was as much a part of the mill as was the whistle. In this burner was consumed what was left of a log after it had been made into boards and timbers. The device was a glutton, but it was necessary. Economics of the time made it so. The minds of lumbermen were then, and properly enough, occupied with how fast and how cheaply the mills could make lumber. So these great, hulking cones, or caged columns of burners, smoldered and flamed by turns and smoked incessantly twenty-four hours daily, consuming un-counted billions of feet of wood that was called "waste." And in those days it *was* waste. But technology caught up.

All of the newer mills have been built without burners, and the burners of most of the older plants now stand idle, relics of an era gone by. There is no need for them now; remarkable progress in machinery and chemistry makes it possible to utilize the whole log—which is all very laudable, but which has removed no little drama from the industry.

A quarter of a century ago, Portland's water front was a tremendous scene at night. From below the city on the Columbia to above Sellwood on the Willamette, the great burners came alive at twilight, glowing sul-lenly, then erupting in smoky flame like so many erratic volcanoes. The illumination was fitful—rising and then fading in brilliance like the Northern Lights. Down the Columbia from Rainier-Longview to Astoria and from Vancouver to Knappton, the waters danced and glowed as the river slid by a score of big sawmills.

Elsewhere, too, it was much the same. On Coos Bay, from Empire to North Bend and Marshfield, the night was alive. Here and there, on both tidewater and in the deepest woods, burners gleamed like lost stars in the dark. This was Wendling or Chiloquin; there was Silverton or Valsetz. Wherever a sawmill stood, there was drama until dawn. We may and do miss the burners, but they were costly and we can afford them no longer.

In terms of wilderness acres, the burnerless operations have saved an infinite forest from being burned wastefully as sawdust instead of being processed as wood briquettes or Presto-Logs and sold as fuel.

A secondary trend in the forest-products industry of late is toward mergers. Small concerns cannot successfully compete for government timber, hence are prone to combine, or simply to quit. Not infrequently mergers result in leaving adrift units that have proved unprofitable, to be sold for junk, and crews that are no longer needed, to be scattered. Oregon is dotted with numerous ghost lumbering towns and logging camps, where men once lived and worked the year around. Today's loggers live in conventional homes with their families and haul their "sticks" to the mills in huge trucks. Here and there, however, is a surviving camp with bunks, bunkhouses, and a cookhouse. The determined visitor to Oregon may be fortunate enough to visit one, perhaps even to have dinner there. There are even a few surviving logging railroads in the Northwest—such as the Longview, Portland and Northern—but they can be counted on the fingers of one hand.

For many years there was no annual jubilee in the state dedicated to forest products—an industry in which Oregon has long led the nation. That need has been filled by the Timber Carnival, staged in July at Albany on the Willamette River. To Albany, for each celebration, come some 50,000 people, who devote three days to whoopee that includes chopping and sawing contests and other sporting events that have grown up in the logging camps since the days when Maine was the nation's top producer of lumber.

Entries still come from Maine and from many more states where the loggers paused when they were cutting the Big Swath across the continent during two centuries. Among the classic events is logrolling, or birling, in which two men stand at opposite ends of a slippery stick of fir or pine, in the water, and each tries to maneuver the log so that he will "wet" the other. Tree-topping is another favorite event, with spurred high-riggers vying to see who can be the quickest to climb a tall Douglas fir, limb it, and then, with a saw, send the top crashing to the ground. All contests are carefully timed and recorded, and cash prizes are awarded along with documents proclaiming the recipient Champion Log-Birler of the World or Champion Tree-Topper.

The gusto of the onlookers is something to see. Three days and nights of bedlam distinguish the Timber Carnival as the liveliest festivity of the season. There is nothing quite like it elsewhere in the United States.

Abandoned sawmills and lumber towns seem to lack the legendary aura that often makes a played-out mining town attractive to tourists. Oregon, which has many such ghost towns, also has its quota of empty mining towns, which testify to the similar emptiness of nearby diggings.

In the production of all kinds of minerals, the state at this writing stands at the bottom of the list so far as the Pacific Northwest is concerned. In terms of millions of dollars, Oregon produced 48.1 worth in 1961, but most of it was sand, gravel, and lava rock. Even Washington's figure, 66.0, was higher, and western Montana, with its copper mines, was at the top with 182.0. But what is said to be the only active nickel mine in the United States is located at Riddle in Douglas County, Oregon, where a smelter is operated.

As for the future, the major population pattern of the Pacific Northwest would seem now to be clearly established. The areas of agricultural potential in the Willamette-Puget Sound lowland and the valleys will always carry the greatest concentrations. However, some new areas will develop as more irrigation projects are completed and a few new communities may spring up as a result of major dam construction and hydroelectric-power production.

In the recent past, federal power has had a noticeable effect in attracting some electro-process industries, such as aluminum, to both Oregon and Washington. But the bulk of low-cost electricity from the federal dams goes to Washington because public agencies have preference and Oregon has relatively few public agencies to take federal power. In any event, it seems probable that, with more irrigation, the Snake River Valley will become one of the major gateways to the western lowlands of the Pacific Northwest.

No arm of the sea, like Washington's Puget Sound, penetrates the important lowland of Oregon to afford favorable urban sites. Instead, the north-flowing Willamette River is the focus of many settlements. The observer is soon aware of the contrast between cities of the two states. Willamette Valley towns are more evenly and closely spaced, appear more mature with their tree-lined streets, and have an intangible New England atmosphere. Agricultural market centers are dominant.

Two factors loom large in the economy of Oregon's future: the steady increases, in both over-all volume and number, of different products of the forest, and tourism.

Every year, out-of-state tourists coming to Oregon outnumber the permanent residents. Most of them, of course, come for sight-seeing or some kind of sporting recreation. The state is admirably equipped to provide them with both.

I trust that, without being too much of a booster, I have conveyed some idea of the scenic enticements. The pictures here should do the rest. As for recreation, sports fishing flourishes in Oregon; and with some of the best big-game hunting anywhere, along with grouse and quail shoot-

Timberline Lodge, located at 6000-foot level on Mt. Hood, is the Pacific Northwest's premier year-round skiing resort.

ing, the state has achieved a reputation as a nimrod's paradise. In a recent issue of a national magazine, reference was made to the therapeutic value of this fortunate part of the country, where people "have the balm of mountains and spring skiing" and where there are fields bursting with "the hidden lure of topknot quail and rivers of glistening trout."

Indeed, the writer of this article wondered why the Pacific Northwest, with nearly one-tenth of the land area of the United States, had attracted but one per cent of its people. Further, he asked, "Why is the population growth in Washington advancing at a rate only slightly higher than that

Mt. Hood offers "the balm of mountains and spring skiing."　　EDWIN J. DOLAN

of the country as a whole, while Oregon's growth was two per cent *lower* than the national average?"

To explain these vital matters, Oregon boosters, both native and acquired, appear to believe that their prototypes resemble the traditional New Englander in that those who "run the state" have made their pile and are no longer interested in a vigorous promotion of the state's economy and institutions. This is, of course, a *status quo* charge one can hear elsewhere; but here it is often hitched to another complaint: that many young people leave Oregon for more lucrative jobs in industry elsewhere, so that "Oregon is educating the technical labor force for California and Washington."

During the decade that ended in 1950, when Oregon enjoyed one of the highest rates of population increase in the country, the public-school system was hard put to keep up with educational demands. However, it proved equal to the task. In fact, even during the depression it was never in danger of the temporary bankruptcy that bedeviled so many states and forced teachers to accept scrip of dubious value. The state's higher education system has survived with unimpaired credit, although the halls of its six colleges become more crowded every year.

Oregon also has a number of private colleges of high repute. Outstanding among them is Reed College, which has been mentioned but deserves a special nod. Its student body of approximately 750 turns out the highest proportion of graduates receiving Ph.D.s in the nation and averages one Rhodes Scholar for every 73 male graduates. Reed has no football team, a grave violation of American college tradition that for 40-odd years has caused grumbling among conventional educators and laymen. The University of Oregon and Oregon State University, however, besides being sound academic citadels, do very well at holding up the state's athletic side.

If, as indicated, tourism offers the best immediate possibilities for boosting Oregon's economy, should not the state make greater efforts to increase the some $200,000,000 which out-of-state visitors spend here annually? Our pro-tourist factions believe that more national forest and state park facilities are needed—things like campsites, picnicking grounds, and such—that the unique moving dunes along the coast should become part of the national park system, and that the high mountain country be left in wilderness status. But another faction asks: How many Oregonians really *want* more tourists? Here one stumbles against a question that seems endlessly in debate.

Politically, Oregon is traditionally conservative, as we have seen, though it has a mixed Republican-Democratic voting record. Until 1954 the state rarely sent a Democrat to Congress. In that year, Richard L. Neuberger broke a forty-year tradition by defeating the Republican candidate for a senate seat. Senator Wayne Morse, elected as a Republican for two terms, deserted the party in 1952 and temporarily became an independent; in 1956 he ran as a Democrat and won re-election. In the State Legislature the two parties seem to be fairly even, with the Democrats in recent years usually taking the lower house and the upper generally being nearly balanced. However, the Democrats are often split into liberal and conserv-

Unique moving dunes near Florence, a proposed national seashore area.

ative factions and the line-up is confused, to say the least. The state has had but one Democratic governor in recent decades, and he lasted only half a term.

Oregon is sound fiscally. We have operated with surpluses, spurned a sales tax or cigarette tax, but we do have a high personal income tax. There has been relatively little political corruption in recent years; but there is a general apathy that prevents the area from landing the big government contracts which, since the war years, have made Washington and California so prosperous.

It is generally admitted that the conservatism of Oregon creates a morally healthy and sound place to live but perhaps not a forward-looking one. Hence the saying, "Oregon is prone to build for yesterday, not for today or tomorrow."

In one area, however, Oregon is as progressive and unparsimonious as its neighboring states: it has never permitted highway construction to lapse. Seemingly, not even school money is more sacred in this automotive era. Highway funds are spent as fast as possible on roads that will "get you there quicker," and the local citizen, as well as the visitor, demands that the shortest distance between two points be the proper measure, no matter what is seen or not seen along the way.

Thus, when on the new super-roads, called freeways, which are designed to relieve congestion on common highways, you never know at a given moment where you are. The best you can do is keep one eye on the road map and the other ready to watch for the exit numbers. No matter what they are named, the freeways do not really run through Oregon or Washington or any other state. They operate in a kind of never-never land—a country of mixed meridians, false creeks, and Big Rock Candy Mountains, all plastered with hideous billboards. For miles you pass through countryside as strange to you as the Gobi Desert or the canal regions of Mars. Then, rising abruptly out of the ground, will appear an improbable mass of buildings, still unrecognizable, still nameless, until an exit sign blocks your vision to say "Hood River, one-half mile." And it *is* Hood River! You got there via the new water-level route that caused the wonderfully scenic old Columbia River highway to be bricked shut as a dangerous nuisance. And you got there fast, with a compelling turnpike speed that makes the swiftly passing scene a panoramic blur to numb the senses, as if the road were bordered on each side by an endless picket fence. And every few years some of these thruways are widened—from two to four to six lanes.

Figuratively, these highways lead into a future for Oregon that will assuredly be much faster paced than the life on the rutted trails the pioneers took. The highways lengthen and straighten, the cities expand, the dams multiply, and the industries grow. The older resident is amazed that all this came out of the wilderness in a few short decades. But, like most Oregonians, he also knows that if care is not taken, if the balance is not preserved between natural and man-made things, these civilized wonders can, in a few short years, destroy—as they have already destroyed along much of the Oregon coast—many of the things that make the incomparably scenic Oregon country so cherished by its inhabitants and its visitors, and in the end create another and no less harsh kind of wilderness.

WASHINGTON

Nard Jones

Mt. Rainier, highest in the Cascades, dominates the landscape of western Washington.

THE first American home in what is now Washington State was established on the Walla Walla River in 1836.

The shelter of a missionary couple, Dr. Marcus Whitman and his wife Narcissa, was not a log cabin. It was a lean-to encompassing with adobe an area thirty by thirty-six feet and roofed with mud and boughs. There on the evening of March 14, 1837, a daughter was born to the devout pair.

Little Alice Clarissa drowned in the river before she was two, and the Whitmans' dream of converting the Cayuse savages ended in tragedy. But this was the first family, these were the first true Washingtonians. That is one reason why in the rotunda of the nation's Capitol you see a statue of Marcus Whitman representing the forty-second state of the Union.

Thus the seed of Washington was planted in martyrdom; and the tradition persists that it was watered by the slavery question. The pioneer who became the symbol of that issue, however, was no slave.

George W. Bush was a freeborn Pennsylvania Negro, and it is almost certain that he paused at the Whitman Mission on his way to the Willamette Valley in the emigration of 1844–45. That wagon train was terribly late, delayed by deep snow in the Blue Mountains, and it seemed to Narcissa Whitman that almost every family needed aid of some kind. But a deeper difficulty was in store for Bush at the end of the Oregon Trail. He found that the Provisional Government forbade the residence of Negroes within its practical jurisdiction. That this law was more political than racist did not lessen its effect for Bush.

He belonged to a group of five families and two bachelors who had elected to stay together in the new land. In this fraternal bond, forged on the long trek, were two Southerners, Michael Simmons and John R. Jackson. Bush's problem seems to have been a reason for the decision of this loyal pair to do some scouting north of the Columbia.

They returned with exciting news about the Puget Sound country. In the fall of 1845 Jackson staked out a claim on the Cowlitz River. A few months later Simmons led a band of Washingtonians-to-be toward a waterfall on the Deschutes River, near where the river emptied into the Sound.

Before the pioneers could hack out settlements on the shores of Puget Sound, they had to reduce the sylvan giants to stumps.   WEYERHAEUSER TIMBER CO.

Simmons called his settlement Newmarket, and George Bush claimed flatland nearby. Bush developed a productive farm, and this took some husbandry, for the Hudson's Bay men were not generous with seed that could be the start of this firmly seated American occupation. They had observed the trend south of the Columbia.

Bush had food to share the next year with the newest emigrants. He refused money, saying they could repay in kind when they were as settled as he. But the Samaritan of Bush Prairie was repaid in more than kind: inevitably the time arrived when late-comers tried to force him off his land because he was a Negro. However, the uprising on his behalf by earlier Puget Sounders was immediate and effective.

Mike Simmons soon established himself as the Puget country's first industrialist, harnessing the power of the falls to a flour mill and then a sawmill. In 1846 the Puget Sounders were almost too occupied themselves to note the end of "joint occupancy" as Britain relinquished claim to the Oregon Country and agreed to a boundary at the forty-ninth parallel. Certainly these first Washingtonians were not surprised at this turn of events: if they had not believed the land would be American, they would not have been there.

In the fall of 1847, however, came news to which the settlers listened most attentively. If the British had given up, the red men had not. Down the Columbia and up to Puget Sound sped fearful word that Narcissa and Marcus Whitman and others at their mission had been murdered by Cayuse.

This development not only closed the interior to settlement for some years but also discouraged many outlanders who had been thinking of free land north of the River of the West. Then something more happened to distract attention from Puget Sound: gold was discovered in California. For a brief time the Oregon Country began to lose some of its sparse population.

But not all the prospectors struck it lucky, and by 1849 most of the Oregonians and Puget Sounders had straggled back. They found no longer an "Oregon Country" but an official Territory. They were relieved to learn that the Indian uprising seemed to be petering out, that a few symbolic culprits had been apprehended and, in due course, would be hanged— after a fair trial, of course.

Again the population of Puget Sound began to pick up. The first Oregon Territory census in 1849 showed only 304 whites north of the Columbia. A year later there were more than 1000, and taking shape near Newmarket were vague outlines of Olympia, the city that would become the capital of an inevitable separate Territory of Washington.

In 1851 claims were ventured farther north. The first white settlers arrived on Whidbey Island, and on the mainland Port Townsend was founded. In September of the same year four men came exploring the Sound, frankly on the lookout for a site that would encourage commerce with the world. Unimpressed by a fledgling agricultural settlement on the Duwamish River, they decided on Alki Point (now West Seattle) in Elliott Bay. David Denny sent a message to his brother Arthur, waiting in Portland, urging him to bring the whole party north.

The others arrived November 13, 1851, in the schooner *Exact*. Later Puget Sounders do not find it astonishing that the record says the skies were pouring heavily as the *Exact's* boat carried the Denny party ashore at "New York Alki," which in Chinook jargon means "Manhattan by and by." A liking for Puget-country rain is an acquired characteristic. The ladies of the party stretched muslin across some bushes, sat down under it, and cried. They were, alas, wearing sunbonnets.

The men of this Illinois party found themselves in business even before they could build shelters. A ship arrived wanting piling for San Francisco wharves, and the infant community allowed that it could oblige. The cargo was furnished, but in the process it was found that a deeper harbor was a necessity. With a clothesline weighted by a horseshoe (though no horse had yet appeared in the region) they sounded the bay more carefully. What they wanted for a harbor was on the eastern shore, across from Alki, and there on February 15, 1852, Arthur Denny and his associates marked their claims.

Less than two months later, on another part of the Sound, Nicholas De Lin and friends began to log off some land. On Commencement Bay, within view of the great mountain the Indians called Takomah, De Lin built a water-driven mill. Within a year he had shipped 550,000 board feet of lumber to the Golden Gate.

It becomes clear that the founding fathers of Washington State were soberly determined rather than colorful. But now and again an exception appeared, and one such was Dr. David S. Maynard, who considerably accelerated the pace of Seattle when he arrived in April of 1852.

When Maynard was a resident of Olympia his friend Chief Sealth, king of the Suquamps and allied tribes, paddled down the Sound one day to suggest that he move to Elliott Bay. Maynard was attracted, and the merchants of Olympia encouraged the transfer. They admitted his charm, his intelligence, and his boundless energy, which sometimes he stoked with spirits. In Olympia he operated a store, and in those days the general merchandise included whisky. Whenever the doctor was personally reducing the inventory on this item he would slash prices or even give his goods away.

The few citizens of the newer community on Elliott Bay were not too concerned with problems of retail trade. They offered to rearrange their claims to accommodate the doctor. During this business Maynard seems to have been in a period of euphoria. Normally not acquisitive, he gave one of the Denny party the impression that he "felt himself monarch of all he surveyed, and of all everybody else had surveyed as well."

Yet the replatting proceeded amiably, and it was soon thereafter that the expansive Maynard suggested the town be given a new name, honoring their great friend Chief Sealth. Inasmuch as the guttural "Sealth" was difficult, the name became Seattle. (In many parts of the world it is still difficult and may be heard as "Sēētle.")

On the way across the plains the ubiquitous doctor had wooed and won a widow, neglecting to mention a wife in the East. When Maynard heard that the latter had arrived on a vessel, he made a beeline for the town barber shop, where he is alleged to have demanded, "Fix me up attractive. I am about to march down the street with a wife on each arm." This he did, and history does not state just how it was that at length the first wife departed in good humor—but she did. Maynard lived to become justice of the peace, notary public, school superintendent, and a member of the convention asking for a separate Territory of Washington.

That separation came on March 2, 1853, when Washington Territory was created by the signature of President Millard Fillmore. Even without the split-off Oregon, the territory was a whopper. It included the land within the present boundaries of the state and parts of what are now Idaho and Montana. (It was not until ten years later that Congress created Idaho Territory and reduced Washington to its present area of nearly 70,000 square miles.)

A controversial little major named Isaac Ingalls Stevens became the first governor. On his way to the newly designated capital of Olympia he employed his journey time making an official survey. Soon he was writing Congress that "a Railroad must be built which will connect our Atlantic seaboard with the coast of Asia via Puget Sound."

Thus, so quickly, Stevens became a cosmopolite of the wilderness, the archetype, perhaps, of a Washingtonian. Why not? Puget Sound was as near to Foochow and Hong Kong as to St. Louis and Chicago. Hawaii seemed more of a neighbor than Boston. New Englanders and Southerners and Midwesterners found themselves rubbing shoulders with foreigners who had been attracted by the kinds of work that had to be done. There were Scots and Irish, Scandinavians, Finns and Poles and Yugoslavs. From the other direction came Chinese, Japanese, and Hawaiians.

At once Governor Stevens set about making treaties with the Indians as a first step toward progress. He was proud of his quick work, but it did not insure peace. Some of the tribes had second thoughts after they affixed their marks, and some of those thoughts they translated into action.

The wars which followed the treaty making of 1855 were not serious compared with the bloodshed on the nations's first frontiers or with the bitter encounters on the plains a decade later. But men, women, and children died on both sides, and there was always the fear of torture—and the torture of fear.

Inevitably, one dawn in the winter of 1856, there was the "Battle of Seattle." It was a comic-opera affair at which the settlers themselves laughed later, despite the deaths of a boy and a young man who grew too curious about what was happening. Fortunately, the Navy's *Decatur* was nearby, and she lobbed grapeshot and balls, keeping the savages to the woods behind the town. Half-dressed citizens ran for the blockhouse, a sensible strategy. One nervous pioneer discharged a rifle ball into the hastily piled hair of a lady, who prompty fainted and was thought dead. Another Seattleite discovered he had donned his wife's red flannel petticoat instead of his pants.

Soon there was little danger from Indians in all the wide land of Washington. A few chiefs dreamed of a great alliance between tribes of the coast and those east of the Cascades. But it was only a dream. Peck's *New Guide to the West*, which many a settler owned, was a dream book too, saying: "The small village rises to a spacious town or city . . . substantial edifices of brick . . . colleges and churches are seen. . . ."

The small villages were indeed rising into towns and cities, each with its own dynamic history adding to the whole story of Washington. Vancouver, down on the lower Columbia, had been an industrial complex even as a Hudson's Bay post. Olympia, Seattle, Tacoma, and Port Townsend all began to feel their oats, as the frontier saying went. On the other side of the mountains Spokane and Walla Walla stirred with the urge of Manifest Destiny. Gold discoveries in the interior and the fever of land speculation added to the yeasting. Hardy pioneers attempted to farm the semiarid country east of the Cascades.

Those territorial years—from 1853 to November of 1889—saw swift progress. Between 1860 and 1862 there was a renewed period of emigration when perhaps 25,000 joined the earlier Washingtonians. But the high point of Washington history in the Civil War period was the completion of the transcontinental telegraph line on September 4, 1864.

Two important milestones were reached in 1867 when the Legislature memorialized Congress for statehood and Alaska was purchased from Russia for $7,200,000. The latter was a windfall that altered the Puget Sound country far more than did graduation from territorial status.

Unquestionably, Elisha P. Ferry was the most able of all the territorial governors. The first of his two terms began in 1872. He strengthened the fight for railroads and showed great practical interest in industry and agriculture.

But it was during the governorship of William Newell, in 1881, that the Northern Pacific Railroad coasted slowly down the western slope of the Rockies, touched Spokane, and integrated the region. The population was then 75,000, and it was difficult to find a Washington village which did not believe it was either on the railroad's path or would be chosen as the western terminus. As General Morton Matthew McCarver had foreseen, Tacoma won that prize—and it was not completely forgiven by Seattle and other neighboring cities until well into this century.

We were warming into statehood by then, and in 1889, when we entered as the forty-second state in the union, the frictions of all the excitement were made manifest in great fires. Seattle, Vancouver, Spokane, and Ellensburg all suffered disastrous blazes. The wooden towns of territorial days were beginning to burn, and in their places would rise brick and mortar, then concrete and steel.

The people had not forgotten the manner and ability of Elisha Ferry, and he was elected first governor of the state. But Ferry's health began to fail, and he could not stem the scramble for pork-barrel legislation. Within ten years the population had soared from 75,000 to 357,000. Chief Sealth's city had grown to 43,000. An Army officer had warned early Spokane settlers that a town could never rise there, but now it was a community of 20,000. The new state was booming, and Washingtonians were certain the boom would never end. Then the panic of '93 warned of the need for financial reform. Governor John H. McGraw led the way, and, as a consequence, was not popular.

Nobody will ever know how the administrative ability of Governor John Rankin Rogers might have stood up without the chance discovery of gold in Alaska in 1897, the first year of his term. But Rogers was a remarkable man, though feared "wild" by conservatives. He was propelled into the governor's chair by his "Barefoot Schoolboy Bill," written when he was in the Legislature, which is the foundation of the state's intense, continuing regard for public education. In *The Story of an American Farm* (he wrote a novel too) Rogers advanced his theories of agrarian democracy. He never needed to test those theories, for the steamer *Portland* arrived in Seattle with $800,000 in gold dust and hard times vanished into skies suddenly blue. Without pain, booming again, Washington slid into the present century.

In this seventh decade of that century it is easy to mark the significant

Many early farmers in the semiarid country east of the Cascades gave up when t... water supply failed.

ROBERT TUTT...

happenings. Almost without exception, the really big events were unrecognized as such. Even the exceptions were misinterpreted, as is inevitable in a young state on the make. For example, only a few local philosophers realized what a great thing had transpired when in 1908 Mount Rainier National Park was established, miraculously just two years after the frantic gold rush.

Washington was passive when in 1902 the Federal Reclamation Act was passed and a few feeble irrigation projects were begun in Yakima and Okanogan counties. In 1909 the big excitement was the Alaska-Yukon-Pacific Exposition which, Seattleites felt, put the Queen City and the state "on the map." There followed pleasant years of expansion and construction.

Then in 1917 Washington became preoccupied with a war that was very distant and with "war industries" that appear feeble in retrospect but foreshadowed later economic patterns. In the innocent teens of the century Washington was fascinated by burgeoning shipyards and by Army-operated spruce mills making lumber for aircraft built elsewhere. As a result, a furniture manufacturer named William Boeing angled for a Navy contract for trainer planes.

But far more important then to Washington State, and certainly vital to the boys at the front, was a happening in the dry-land country across the Cascades. Ephrata farmers were about to give up, and they might have except that Uncle Sam said he needed every ounce of food that could be managed. So those farmers stuck it out, encouraged by men like Billy Clapp, and Jim O'Sullivan, and Rufus Woods of Wenatchee. These men were talking about a fabulously big dam on the Columbia that someday would bring water to the sagebrush country.

In 1919, just as the war was over, came the "Seattle Revolution." Actually it was a one-day protest, but it was the first "general strike" (and, thus far, the last) to take place in the U.S.A. Many a Seattle businessman—and many citizens throughout the nation, too—feared it was the beginning of bloody anarchy.

No shot was fired, no club wielded. Shipyard workers and their supporters went back to work, but labor had shown its muscles. Nerves stretched taut, and the Industrial Workers of the World—the I.W.W.s or "Wobblies"—chose the time to do some organizing in the lumber mills and logging camps around Centralia. Washingtonians are still arguing as to whether the "Wobblies" or Legionnaires in an Armistice Day parade precipitated the fight that killed four marchers. The tragic affair was climaxed with a mob's hanging Wesley Everest, who was both an I.W.W. and a veteran. There was bloodshed in Everett, too, when "Wobblies" attempted to land there in a small steamer. Out of it all came better working conditions in the

"New" acres across the Cascades now bloom with apple orchards watered by federal irrigation projects.   WENATCHEE CHAMBER OF COMMERCE

mills and woods and perhaps the seed that makes Washington today one of the strongest "labor states" in the union. However, that generalization is modified by farm sections east of the mountains where organized labor is still weak.

The twenties were what they were for other states—a decade of mild insanity, reminiscent in Washington of the boóm days that trailed statehood. Yet the harshest echoes of the crash reached us tardily, so there was time for huzzas at the completion in 1929 of the longest (7.8 miles) railroad tunnel in the world, through the Cascades.

Then the great depression struck viciously at an economy based almost wholly on lumber and fish. The citizenry was too stunned to take much notice of the first power dam on the Columbia, at Rock Island, a privately financed project. Washington stirred less than Oregon at the completion of the far larger Bonneville, the first federal dam, in 1937. By then prosperity showed signs of returning and Washington was busy recouping. A year later conservatives and the lumber interests grumbled at the establishment of Olympic National Park, although enlightenment was close.

Then in 1942, despite a horrifying war that to most Washingtonians was in the Pacific rather than in Europe, imagination soared again. The Grand Coulee Dam, the biggest thing ever built by man, was completed. It was a symbol of pioneer achievement, the dream of those Ephrata farmers (during another world conflict) come true. The Boeing plant had become a giant arsenal and, with it and the Grand Coulee Dam, Washingtonians felt strongly identified with certain victory. The feeling grew with the mystery of the Hanford Engineering Works, which the big dam had made possible.

By 1953 Washington was still hoping that its new power and its atoms would be used for peace. In that year we celebrated the Territorial Centennial, rather thoughtfully. What we knew for certainties were these things: we had been taking part in world events; our industrial base had grown pleasingly complex but somehow seemed too largely dependent upon world unrest; and another emigration was on, with strangers heading northwest again with the sunset in their eyes.

Across the Cascades "new" acres blossomed where desert had been and more dams were on the way. We were in the path of airliners, as once we had been in the path of covered wagons and sailing ships. If Man was determined to explore outer space—well, Boeing was ready.

Such mid-twentieth-century trappings were new, but the feeling was old and familiar. Restless, stubbornly optimistic as always, Washingtonians felt the urge for some bold move. There was no "further west." But clearly there were frontiers in space and time. That in essence, I think, was what

Boeing planes and Seattle are synonymous.

triggered both the World's Fair and its theme of the World of Tomorrow.

Why not? For a long, long time the state motto had been "Alki"—meaning "by and by."

What of the stage for the events just described?

Washington is roomy enough for even Alaskans to move around in with comfort: 66,836 square miles of land and 1721 square miles of water, facing upon the greatest of oceans. On the vertical it stretches from minus sea level to the 14,410-foot crest of Mount Rainier. On the horizontal it reaches

Sugar-beet plant in desert country of Moses Lake.   BUREAU OF RECLAMATION

237 miles from the Canadian border to the Columbia River and 354 miles west to east, from Cape Flattery to the border of Idaho.

The population is moving close to the 3,000,000 mark. We are proud of that but aren't too certain that we like it. Washington 20 years ago boasted a square mile for every 25 persons. Now there are about 40 persons in that square mile—statistically speaking, of course, because actually about 65 per cent of us live in towns and cities now.

Yet those communities are not what older states would call crowded. And the cities—with roads, parks, and game refuges—take up only 8 per cent of the only state in the union named for a President. About 22 per cent of the land is in pasture and 16 per cent is in crops. About 54 per cent is forest land—and we like to say that the forest is a crop too. Washington invented the "Tree Farm" system back in 1944.

In addition to the two great forested national parks—Rainier and Olympic —there are nine national forests and six state forests. The 1,750,000 acres of state-owned forests are popularly known as "school timber" and are guarded as such for educational purposes.

Such general references to land use do not reflect the infinite variety of Washington State. Its nickname, "Evergreen Land," tells you little, although it is more accurate than it used to be in the days before the big dams and the vast irrigation network.

Generalizations about the climate can also mislead. Walla Walla is on the lee side of the Cascades, as is Spokane, but its average July temperature is sixteen degrees higher, although the rainfall is about the same for the two cities. Out on the wild Olympic Peninsula the town of Sequim (pronounced Skwim) has only sixteen inches of rainfall annually. Forks, relatively nearby, averages 115 inches a year. The explanation is that Sequim is in what we Washingtonians call a "banana belt," although we have yet to raise our first banana.

To make the climate more curiously varied, mix in those great Pacific flows—the Alaska current, the North Pacific current, the California ocean stream—add the prevailing winds plus a few unpredictable ones along the mountain passes, and flavor with the crazy williwaws of lake and river canyons. Top all this with peaks of perpetual snow—and don't forget the glaciers.

In winter months, with this combination, Washington can offer just about any kind of climate you prefer. In summer the choice is narrower: on the west side the days are mild, often sunny, with occasional showers; on the east side the summer is warm to warmer, the nights blessedly cool.

But let us get on to the flora and fauna.

This is indeed the land of the Big Woods, as with British Columbia and Oregon. Long ago we borrowed Paul Bunyan and Babe, the Blue Ox, from the mythical world of Minnesota and beyond, and we intend to keep them. It is difficult for even Washington poets to think of our forests without Paul. It is not easy to forget that Washington ranks third in the nation in lumber and wood products, that the forests bring in something like $300,000,000 a year, and that we are second in the production of wood pulp and sixth in paper and allied products, all of which mean another $250,000,000 or so.

The trees which entranced our practical, transplanted Paul Bunyan in-

The forest crop rolls down out of the mountain to the sawmill in flatcars nearly a half mile long.

clude the giant Douglas fir, which may reach 300 feet into the sky with its straight brown trunk and hanging cones. They also include the hemlock, with the short, flat needles; the sugar pine and ponderosa; and the big, aromatic cedar, from which shingles are made—a nice deep red when new, a beautiful gray after weathering. From those cedars the first Washingtonians made many a brave war canoe, astonishing multifamily dwellings, and a few totem poles as well.

Such trees are only the more dramatic and most useful. For the New Englander homesick for color against the evergreens in autumn, there are

Or in logging trucks.

RAY ATKESON

Washington's big farm crop is wheat. BUREAU OF RECLAMATION

hardwoods: the maple and the oak and the brilliant shrub-vine we call a maple thicket. Crimson is a badge of many a Washington shrub—the Pacific red elder, the Cascade mountain ash, the red mountain heath. Sometimes the splash of color against the dark green is eminently edible, as in huckleberry or wild raspberry.

Those pastures and meadows and croplands have aesthetic value too. Yet even here Paul Bunyan intrudes, for east of the Cascades he is a rancher, not a logger, and in agriculture his storied feats are as great as they are in the woods. Inasmuch as most of us live in the urban areas, rel-

*Steel-pipe sections being loaded on barges in Portland for transportation to an eastern
Washington irrigation project.*   AL MONNER

atively few Washingtonians realize that our farm-produced dollars exceed
the value of forest products by $200,000,000 or $300,000,000. We are first
in apples, third in pears, first in hops and peas, and among the top five
states in prunes, grapes, apricots, and cherries. But the big crop is wheat
—as much as $150,000,000 worth a year, to rank us fifth in the nation.

Even flowers are a crop in Washington. Those vast fields of tulips and
daffodils which delight the tourists in April are really a multimillion-dollar
bulb industry.

If all this practicality shocks you, please note that we do not try to cash in

On this managed land, wood, water, and wildlife (including bears) are produced for present and future generations.   WEYERHAEUSER TIMBER CO.

on our wild flowers. There are at least 1000 species in the Olympic National Park alone. Rhododendron, the state flower, blooms along the coast in late spring. But wild flowers are everywhere: on the mountain meadows, in the scablands of the Columbia's deeper gorges. They bloom in lava desert and in alkali dust and in snowdrifts. Often I have found the wild rose in the untended weeds of a parking lot.

Were I a bona fide bird watcher, instead of a mere gull gazer, I am certain I would love Washington even more than I do. Yet the spiritual descendants of Audubon do not wear such happy smiles as once they did.

They say there are not as many feathered friends hereabouts as there used to be. It is getting difficult even to spot the willow goldfinch, our state bird. But faithfully each year the bird lovers mark the arrival of Steller's jay, the Oregon Towhee, and the junco with his black bonnet. They look for the varied thrush, the red-shafted flicker, and the cedar wax-wing. These are the birds more commonly seen, along with the ubiquitous magpie and crow and robin. In the desert country there is a turkey-necked vulture, not to be recommended as a sight to lift the heart.

As for mammals, it is not true that you may salute a grizzly in Washington State; nor will you encounter a brown bear. That bear with the brownish fur is a black bear, if I make myself clear. Sometimes he really *is* black, and often he will appear friendly. Wise foresters advise you to take no stock in his overtures; and you will do his breed no favor by feeding him.

I have never seen a cougar or a mountain goat in Washington, but both are here. To have glimpsed elk and black-tailed deer is nothing to brag about. There are highway signs warning you to watch out for them, and the signs mean what they say.

If you roam Washington widely enough, you are certain to see a white-tailed jack rabbit or hear a marmot whistle. If you are unarmed, you may glimpse a coyote atop some lonely hill, but gun metal he can smell. Any Washingtonian worthy of the name has surprised a raccoon surprising a frog and heard a beaver slide into a stream with an angry hiss.

Puget Sounders boast that there are no poisonous snakes in the region; but those who live on the east side of the state are quieter on the subject. This is due to the Pacific rattler, not one of which has ever seen the Pacific. Against scabrock or prairie he is hard to detect, but he does warn with his rattles as he coils to strike. It is a sound that you will somehow recognize even the first time.

You have heard of the fighting salmon in Washington State waters, and probably all that you have heard is true. What the stranger may not know is that in recent years the commercial fisherman and the sports fisherman and the Indian with his treaty rights have been quarreling about the fisheries increasingly.

This can mean only one thing: that there does not seem to be quite enough fish for everybody. Nobody knows for a certainty just how many fish the sportsmen and Indians are taking, although reasonable guesses are made. It is a matter of record that the annual commercial catch is about 125,000,000 pounds in a good year, that the value is something like $20,000,000, and that Washington ranks seventh among states for the value of its fisheries.

The sports fishermen claim that theirs is a big industry, too, when you

Steelhead return from distant ocean to spawn in a sparkling mountain stream.
WEYERHAEUSER TIMBER CO.

add in the costs of boats and gear and trailers and gasoline. It is fortunate for all of us that somebody is remembering the fish in the dispute. We will all be better off when more attention is paid to the findings and advice of the great School of Fisheries at the University of Washington and to the brilliant research of the U. S. Fish and Wildlife Service and Washington Department of Fisheries. For our fish problem is now complicated by another factor—the increased offshore fishing of Russia and Japan.

Being in the shadow of Roderick Haig-Brown, who will be with you presently, I am not going to try to tell you anything about fish. He knows the sea salmon as he knows the rainbow or cutthroat, the Dolly Varden, the bass and perch. I will only add that from the upper Columbia and the lower Snake the fisherman still drags forth an occasional sturgeon weighing nearly half a ton.

Catching the giant goeduck (gweduc)—we pronounce it gooey-duck—would not be classed as a sport by my old friend of Campbell River. It is rather stupid, even for a clam. It feeds so heavily that it reaches a weight of five or six pounds and cannot get into its shell. Although it is not a handsome shellfish, many Washingtonians find it highly palatable.

But it cannot compare as food with the Dungeness crab, our razor clams, or the Olympia and Quilcene and Willapa oysters. Or our tiny Pacific shrimp. And now we are experimenting with oyster species imported from Japan.

Of course, not all of us haunt the shore merely to eat. Some of us are sea lion watchers. And along the beaches and in the tide pools are beautiful creatures which are a delight to children and to adults with the eyes and wonder of a child.

Our seacoast is down on the map as 157 miles in length, but a man could spend a lifetime exploring the Olympic Peninsula, Juan de Fuca Strait and Puget Sound and the hundreds of bays and inlets and channels. Stretch the state's shore lines as straight as a string and that cord would reach down past Oregon and beyond the southern boundary of California, too.

Probably no other state of all the fifty can boast such variegation. Experts in physiography divide Washington neatly into seven parts. The seven faces of Washington are the Olympic Mountains, the Willapa Hills, the Puget Sound Basin, the Cascades, the Okanogan Highlands, the Columbia Basin, and the Blue Mountains. Even the most hurried tourist observes that these areas are indeed quite distinct.

Washingtonians are only now beginning to take proper pride in our open spaces and trying to preserve them. Hardly a week goes by that I don't hear some welcome newcomer from the heavily populated East say, "Here there's room to hunt and fish and roam, and not far away."

Comparatively speaking, yes. But we who have been here longer can remember easily how there was much more room in which to roam, and even closer by. We listen more attentively than of old when, for example, there is serious talk of preserving the northern Cascades area as a national park and when conservationists recommend a Wilderness Area on the seacoast. A few decades ago many of us were fearful that the terrible Harold Ickes intended to throw the whole Olympic Peninsula into a federal park. Now almost every community club flies to arms when logging "a little" of the Olympic National Park is mentioned.

The forest hugs the sea along the rugged Olympic Peninsula coast.

WASHINGTON STATE DEPT. OF COMMERCE

We know it was inevitable that vast landscapes had to vanish first before the ax, then the plow, and finally the city. We know what happens to the mammals and the fishes, the plants and the waters, and the air, as a result. We have seen the highways grow from two lanes to four, then six and eight, and we hear the engineers talk of twelve lanes—and we are filled with wonder. But it is not always the kind of wonder the engineers believe they have inspired in us.

Of course we know that we cannot make Washington look as it once did. Most of us realize now that we can only hope to keep as much of it as possible, keep it as it is now, and with luck reclaim some more of it.

We know that our 3,000,000 people will become 4,000,000, and sooner than we think. And that our 68,557 square miles of water and land will not expand.

Traditionally the logger and the commercial fisherman have been the archetypes in Washington State. In reality they are giving way to the makers of jetliners and the space engineers, to the builders of highways and bridges and dams. We have already noted how the farmers, although decreasing in number, increase in stature by the values of their products.

A quick glance at how we make our livings tells the story. The vast majority of employable Washingtonians—between 180,000 and 200,000—are in manufacturing. Most of the manufacturing is done in the Puget Sound area. And in the so-called Greater Seattle Area 53 per cent of the factory jobs are accounted for by missile and aircraft and satellite production. Statewide, about 29 per cent of the factory jobs have to do with defense, as compared with somewhat less than 23 per cent in California and somewhat over 21 per cent in Connecticut.

The figures have never been satisfactorily broken down, but what we know does suggest that a very high percentage of the approximately 180,000 engaged in trade are in turn greatly dependent upon the income from those engaged in defense and missiles and aircraft.

Against these figures, those employed by farming, forestry, and fisheries combined muster not more than around 80,000 or 90,000. Almost as many as that are busy in professional services or in transportation, communication, and utilities. Those who have seen our subdivisions burgeoning on hill and dale will not be astonished that nearly 40,000 of us are in finance, insurance, and real estate. Curiously, not 10,000 are making a livelihood in recreational services, but that is a fast-growing category now. And so is government—municipal, county, state and federal.

How we keep the wolves at bay does not tell much about the kind of people we are. Are Washingtonians different from our neighbors in other

Many sawmills are located in the forest.

areas of the Pacific Northwest? Certainly our neighbors to the north are inclined to think so. Western Canadians find us politically naïve and unduly addicted to the profit system. Yet British Columbians like to visit us, and we enjoy having them, and certainly the province is a favorite vacation region of Washingtonians. We meet symbolically once a year at the Blaine Peace Arch to remind ourselves that ours is one of the few peaceful, unguarded international boundaries left in the world.

It seems to me that the folks of Idaho and Montana are perhaps more philosophical than Washingtonians and that they have a keener sense of

The Blaine Peace Arch stands at the border of Washington and British Columbia.

WILLIAMS BROS.

humor. The broad frontier spirit is still extant in those states, while we in the transition stage find it more awkward to poke fun at ourselves.

As for Oregonians, I have found them more seasoned than Washingtonians. That would be natural; their history is a bit longer, and that history has been less accidental than ours. The old sectional rivalry persists, but in a new way. The dynamism of eastern Washington's industries and its "agribusiness" flows down the Columbia into the area of Oregon that is the most heavily populated and the most influential politically. Except for Vancouver and Longview, the Washington towns south of Olympia feel keenly the pull of Oregon. The highways are fast and Oregon has liquor on Sundays and no sales tax, in addition to other attractions. There are Puget Sounders who regard such phenomena with distaste. They ask plaintively why we should build fine highways in order to drain business out of our state—and spend federal money on the River of the West, which neatly avoids Tacoma and Seattle.

It should be added that there are wise Oregonians who are also less than happy about this unavoidable situation. These see a quiet way of life passing in older Oregon. My good friend Stewart Holbrook is among this school, and I sympathize with him.

In attempting to understand Washingtonians, it is necessary to keep in mind the youthfulness of the state. When you read here of the passing of some distinguished gentleman of ninety-two or so, you read also in the obituary a capsule history of Washington. In the year of his birth there were no more than three dwellings on the whole shore line of Lake Washington. The owners reached the village of Seattle over an Indian trail through a virgin forest. Anacortes was hardly more than a place where whalers careened their vessels to rid them of barnacles.

It cannot be expected that a state so young will have produced people who know themselves, as do New Englanders and Virginians. We understand this and make no apologies for it, because we realize that time will improve us. But we feel deeply for bewildered newcomers in this matter. They come prepared to like us, and even to be like us. Often they grow discouraged. How can you find out about people in the process of finding out about themselves? It is, I think, our paradoxes which are most baffling to the stranger.

In the field of politics we carry on the most spirited partisan campaigns, then take ourselves to the voting machines to cross party lines with an abandon that quite literally has abetted suicide among our more sensitive politicians. We think nothing of electing a Democratic governor and giving him a predominantly Republican Legislature with which to struggle—or choosing a Republican governor to the accompaniment of a strongly Demo-

Seattle water front, with Mt. Rainier in the background.   FRED MILKIE

cratic body of lawmakers in Olympia. Through decades of this century we consistently sent Democrats to the U. S. Senate and sped Republicans to the House of Representatives.

When the green curtain of the voting machine is drawn, we are utterly unpredictable, be the issue a school levy or a dog-leash law. Often there will be nothing in the campaign to give the pundits an advance clue as to our behavior on election day.

There are periods when we hanker for a little entertainment on the part of candidates and officeholders. This euphoria is usually followed by a conscientious effort to choose the dullest and most colorless aspirants on view. Once upon a time Seattle elected a mayor who promised a return to the wild, gay spirit of Alaska's gold-rush days. He was elected, and he fulfilled his promise with enthusiasm. Then, when the time came for his re-election, Seattleites decided they wanted the city closed up, and our hero—suitably named Hi Gill—went down to defeat. Knowing his constituency, he simply bided his time. On the third time around he promised a municipal government fully approved by the clergy. Seattle knew he was a man of his word, returned him to office, then sat back piously to watch results. Mr. Gill's assistants padlocked prostitution, confiscated gambling gear, and splintered speak-easy furniture with axes. Everybody was happy except Mr. Gill's old cronies.

Still today we cast sheep's eyes occasionally at the more robust night life of cities in other states. As the World's Fair came on, and we seemed to be getting a broader nocturnal activity, several segments of the population grew nervous. But when an effort was made to modify the interpretation of our 1909 "Blue Laws," which prohibit Sunday liquor, the idea died a-borning.

It is often pointed out that our church activities are many and the money for new religious edifices is limitless. It is true that in numbers of sects we seem to be vying with Los Angeles. At last count there were sixty-two denominations; a few boasted no more than fifty members and one church, but all are growing.

That is only part of the story, the part that frightens politicians. Our actual church membership is only 30 per cent, lowest among all states of the Union. One sizable denomination seriously considered returning Washington to the category of "foreign mission."

Our paradoxes are small as well as large. We love our ferry boats and proudly advertise them to the world—while we build ever more bridges, which will make the ferries a part of the past.

We write ecstatically of the romance of our halibut fleet, but the best market for its product are the fish stalls of the Eastern Seaboard. Our highest gastronomic praise is reserved for King Salmon baked fresh, yet most of us know him only in the tin, and our school children prefer tuna—a regrettable state of affairs.

We defend our climate passionately. But almost every Washingtonian who can afford the money and the time spends as many months as possible at Palm Springs or Tucson or Phoenix or in Honolulu. A sun tan has become a status symbol in Washington as elsewhere, but our prodigal sons return affirming that—take it all year 'round—Washington has the best damned climate in the world.

We are a family people, and although we are vocally proud of our increasing number of fine restaurants, only 6 per cent of us furnish those cafés with more than 90 per cent of their business. Our entertaining is mostly in the home. We like to think of ourselves as outdoor people—much on the road, on the mountaintop, on the bank of a fishing stream, on the trail of a deer, and, of course, on the patio.

Yet also we see ourselves as endorsing culture, even appreciating it. There is the evidence that Seattle supports a symphony orchestra, and so do some Washington cities the size of Walla Walla. When a road show or concert or lecturer arrives, we gather enough people together to make an audience. Not long ago this imposed a strain on a rather small minority. But transplanted Boeing engineers and an increasing number of teachers (the University of Washington is now the second largest employer in Seattle) make the cultural going easier now.

Not the least of the Puget Sound country's interest in the World's Fair was the fact that it would leave a permanent science pavilion, opera house and theater. For a relatively new state, we have remarkable galleries and museums, and our public library system is a matter of pride. When it comes to the outright purchase of books, we are improving at an amazing rate. A Seattle suburb of 30,000 people has a small bookshop which grosses more than $85,000 a year—unheard of in Washington 10 years ago.

Per capita we produce more than our share of writers, musicians, dancers, artists, and poets. Once upon a time there were thousands of Washingtonians writing poetry about the scenery, but we have passed into a more sophisticated stage. At the University of Washington there is a group of young poets who have attracted wide attention, and the brilliant Theodore Roethke may be said to be the spiritual leader.

A few years ago Pacific Northwest artists, like the earlier poets, were intensely regional. Today there are several Washington artists who have transcended regionalism—a very difficult thing where nature is so imposing. Such men as Mark Tobey and Morris Graves had to exhibit elsewhere before most Washingtonians began to understand and appreciate their work. Eustace Zeigler and Ernest Norling are among those who chose to stay rooted and interpret the Washington scene literally.

We are a long way from Manhattan and Hollywood, even in the jet age, so that most of our more gifted dancers, musicians, and actors must leave home for audiences and patrons. But the little-theater movement, which has long flourished in Washington, is offering wider opportunities. Glenn Hughes of the University of Washington pioneered the theater-in-the-round and the so-called "penthouse" theater.

Washington has many more book authors than it had twenty-five years

University of Washington campus in Seattle.   JAMES O. SNEDDON

ago. The annual Pacific Northwest International Writers Conference, held at Seattle, takes on some of the aspects of an industrial convention. Yet the record seems to show that somehow we do not yet have a "writing climate." Many of our writers have produced their best work after they have moved away. H. L. Davis was a shining example of the Washington writer who had to stand off a few thousand miles in order to do the region justice, and he was perhaps the nearest thing to a writing genius the state has yet produced. Yet there are exceptions enough to confuse the generality that Washington's writing climate is weak. Betty MacDonald emerged fully equipped with her wholly indigenous *The Egg and I* and posthumously continues to hold a wide national audience. James Stevens and Archie Binns are novelists of solid accomplishment, and Murray Morgan is bringing a fresh note to the region's nonfiction. Jack Leahy and George Bluestone, both on the faculty of the University of Washington, are among the younger writers who show fine promise.

Aside from those who have achieved recognition in specific fields, Washington has lacked citizens of broad national renown. Here again it is noticeable that many of our best-known natives have found their niches far away. Ralph Cordiner, born near Walla Walla, had to seek Manhattan in order to become chairman of the General Electric Board. It is doubtful that William O. Douglas would have been quite so famous as a Wenatchee lawyer as he is in his robe of justice of the Supreme Court.

Yet you must travel far in Washington to find a businessman who would trade places with Cordiner or a lawyer who would give up Washington State for Washington, D.C., and national fame. There are plenty of opportunities here, and it cannot be said that our businessmen and professional men do not make the most of them.

When we observe the success of businesses and professions in Washington State, we encounter another paradox. Our business and agricultural leaders most firmly and soberly endorse private enterprise. At a chamber of commerce meeting in Tacoma or Pullman they will applaud vigorously the speaker who enshrines competition and deplores the inroads of public ownership. But, in doing so, they appear innocent of information that a great deal of the state's progress and prosperity must be credited to the big federal and PUD dams and the industry, agriculture, and river commerce they attract or create. The effects of government contracts, of course, are deeply known by the supermarket operator as well as by the owner of the corner grocery. Curiously, Washington businessmen are seldom heard on the subject unless there is danger of losing some of this support of "big government."

Thus cynics are heard to say that the Washington economy would be in a bad way "if peace should break out in the world." True, the withdrawal symptoms would be particularly painful, but the cynics are unfair in assuming that private enterprise in Washington has no program looking toward a truly peacetime era.

By invitation the state government joins the annual pilgrimage of businessmen to the East and Midwest, where efforts are made to convince distant tycoons that they should build plants or branches in Washington. This campaign for new industries is a steady one and is sharpened by area rivalries within the state. Boeing, the giant, is sensitive to its responsibilities for the future. It is not generally known that the company employs many "idea men" whose job is to sit in cubicles and dream up markets and products that have little to do with aircraft and moon shots.

Tacoma claims Mt. Rainier as its protective mountain.   TACOMA CHAMBER OF COMMERCE

Washington missionaries who travel eastward seeking new industries encounter hazards. Many eastern capitalists still remember the jibe, usually attributed to Jim Farley, that there were "forty-seven States, and the Soviet of Washington." We regard this as a stale canard matched only by the rumor that it rains continuously here.

In politics, as has been suggested already, our elections are not necessarily a reflection of a general political climate. Washington began as a Democratic state and, except for a conservative reaction in the twenties, has continued to be Democratic in spirit. The Populists were very strong in Washington State in the nineties. In 1912, when Woodrow Wilson was elected President, voters in the Evergreen Land cast 40,000 votes for Eugene V. Debs, the Socialist candidate, against 86,000 for Wilson. But you get a sharper focus on that election when you observe that Theodore Roosevelt captured 113,000 ballots.

The state's love affair with the early New Deal was spectacular (and produced some spectacular politicians), and once upon a time the Townsendites were influential. So were the Technocrats. The notorious Commonwealth Federation in the thirties showed an influence alarming to both Democrats and Republicans. But that strength was temporary. The initial impact of a vocal protesting minority can usually be felt in Washington.

Our increasing tribes of millionaires and well to do have not found this history a serious deterrent, even as they exercise their right to deplore it. Cannily they understand that often such political manifestations are more apparent than real in any sensible political examination of Washington State.

Stop a hundred Washingtonians on the street and ask them to comment, one by one, on private ownership in industry and a very large majority will endorse it. But bring those hundred together in a meeting place and a vote for a specific *public* operation may pass by almost the same majority. At their core, for example, both Seattle and Tacoma are capitalistic cities, yet each is intensely proud of its successful, municipally owned power and light and feels that it pioneered low-cost electricity in the region. Port Angeles had a city electric system as early as 1893, and there are twenty-two Public Utility Districts in the state. Public-power enthusiasts submit that these operations, plus federal power, account for the low-cost electric energy so important to the commonwealth. The three private power companies naturally contest this uncomplicated view, and it is noticeable that today there is a practical working arrangement among all types of utilities in the state.

There is no question that the state's great river system has contributed to the liberality of the political view. More than half the power produced in the whole Pacific Northwest is generated at federal dams and is marketed

Grand Coulee Dam, largest on the continent, is the fruit of the state's love affair with the early New Deal.

through the Bonneville Power Administration; about 14 per cent comes from private companies in Washington. Yet those companies serve nearly two-fifths of the state's customers for electricity. In a state of many broad rural sections it should be noted that the public agencies have made electrification possible in areas as yet impractical for the private companies.

If on the long pull Washington has been liberal and progressive, it has never been more liberal or more progressive than the nation of which it is a part. In short, it has always been willing to pioneer in ideas, but not in ideologies.

Our record on racial discrimination is not perfect, but is by no means shameful. The riots against the Chinese in the nineties were the product of railroad building and financial panic. They were firmly suppressed by the most conservative element. The later deportation of the Japanese was a product of war hysteria and was never entered into in Washington with enthusiasm. The Negro was a rarity in the state prior to World War II; his appearance after that was sudden and in sizable numbers. There have been no serious incidents, although the Urban League does not feel that assimilation has been sufficiently rapid. In Seattle the NAACP has charged that, despite state laws, segregation is covertly severe as to housing and hiring. There is no school segregation, but the Association points out that the housing situation creates what are virtually all-Negro schools.

It is the frontier tradition to take pride in a classless society. The nearest thing to a social "set" is the Tacoma group which for three generations has ridden to hounds, not a generally popular sport in Washington. It has been several decades since residents of Seattle's First Hill tried to keep their social events out of the papers and upstarts out of their social events.

The nearest approach to an aristocracy has been achieved somewhat unwittingly by the masters and mistresses of the great wheat ranches of the Palouse and Walla Walla country. They are proud of roots deep in the land itself and aware of being pleasantly unrelated to the industrial excitement in the densely populated parts of the state. Their incomes are high, and chemical and mechanical innovations have freed them from the vassalage of the old-time harvests.

Washingtonians as a whole are very much in a period of transition, and I sometimes doubt that we will ever be anything else. We were in transition a quarter of a century ago when only two-fifths of us were native-born. But now young families, with two to half a dozen children each, are reversing that condition. And these young natives may decide, in due course and by their preferences, what *is* exactly a Washingtonian.

In times past I have presumed to suggest to strangers what they should see in Washington State.

Of course I could pretend that you have all the time in the world. Whereupon I would suggest pedantically that you divide your itinerary into seven parts and explore in turn the areas enumerated some pages back. I would urge that you examine all seven faces of Washington: the Olympic Peninsula, the Willapa Hills, the Puget Sound Basin, the Cascades, the Okanogan Highlands, the Columbia Basin, and the Blue Mountains.

But that is quite an order in these busy times. It would be more sensible if I simply implored you to examine parts of *both* sides of the Cascades

Climbers rest on Dome Peak in the North Cascades Wilderness. This area has been proposed for a national park. EDWIN J. DOLAN

Range. A visit to only the Puget Sound country would no more enable you to savor the quality of Washington State than would a visit to only the Inland Empire around Spokane.

I make this simple suggestion and then refer to perhaps the only written passage from my youth that I am willing to stay with now:

"There is only one true approach to such a land. One must be wide-eyed and somewhat haphazard, ready for anything. That was the approach of the explorer, the wanderer, the adventurer. That is the spirit in which the

Space Needle and monorail of Seattle's Century 21 Fair. SEATTLE POST-INTELLIGENCER

Seattle's floating bridge connects Lake Washington with Mercer Island. FRED MILKIE

farthest reach has been met for more than two hundred years. There is nothing wrong with it that I can see."

I do not care to set down any firm guidelines for the newcomer. I would much prefer that out of our great variety you see the things that are right for you alone. If you sense a place partly by palate, as any true gourmet will, then you will find the proper restaurant. If your heart yearns toward the sea and ships, that café will be on one of our teeming water fronts.

In the larger cities I have no worry about your finding the things that are right for you. For a night view Seattle is one of the most beautifully lighted cities in the world. You are certain to be atop the Space Needle

The $20,000,000 state capitol at Olympia.
WASHINGTON DEPT. OF COMMERCE AND ECONOMIC DEVELOPMENT

somewhat after dusk on your first day in Seattle. If modern architecture and new civic centers interest you, there are the permanent buildings the Queen City inherits from the World's Fair.

You will find the giant Boeing complex at Seattle and Renton, the floating bridges across Lake Washington and the Chittenden Locks of the Ship Canal, which join salt water with fresh. You will gaze knowingly (or lubberly) at the hundreds of smart small craft moored at Ballard's huge marina.

Many visit Tacoma just to drive through its beautiful residential sections.

Industrialists come from afar to wonder at the busy tide-flats area with its manufacturing diversification found in no other city in the state. Historians are attracted to the library and archives of the Washington State Historical Museum. Tourists of serious bent are edified at the brilliant exhibits.

You should not drive through Olympia without visiting the Capitol grounds and buildings. I think they are among the most beautiful capital edifices in the United States. They set us back nearly $20,000,000 when the dollar was much harder.

In Spokane it is traditional to meet friends in the lobby of the Davenport Hotel. Puget Sounders drive across the state in spring simply to enjoy the Duncan Gardens there, adding a jaunt to Mount Spokane State Park, from which you look down on a world of lakes and rivers and forests and, of course, progress.

Yes, you'll easily find the things you seek in the cities—the jazz joints that have sprung up along Seattle's old Skid Road, or the "shanghai tunnels" beneath the streets of Port Townsend, or the wonderful pastoral quiet of Walla Walla's City Park. I have known Midwest farmers to fly to the Tri-Cities of Richland, Pasco, and Kennewick—not for the desert scenery, although it is there, but to examine that development which is so big that it can no longer be embraced by the terms agriculture and chemurgy. It throws in the production of pulp and paperboard, and includes the arts of transportation and distribution.

All of this is within the magic circle of the biggest atomic-energy plant in the world. Doubtless by the time of your visit there'll be under way a plant to harness 800,000 kilowatts from steam that was wasted. Richland is the government town that was transformed into an independent community. It is the Town of War that has become a Town of Peace, inviting tourists with its soft, warm climate. Pasco and Kennewick are the once sleepy farm trading villages which, with Richland, have come to be the center of the fastest-growing area in the state.

Those itinerant Midwest farmers, if they are as observing as most of their kind, will not fail to note the big roles played in Washington State by the U. S. Corps of Engineers and the Bureau of Reclamation. The Columbia Basin Project is the most ambitious reclamation program in the United States—2,500,000 acres, nearly half of which have been found suitable to irrigation. One of the great wonders of the state is embraced in that network of tunnels and canals, of siphons and prehistoric watercourses, bringing water from Lake Roosevelt, behind Grand Coulee Dam. It covers a sprawling land eighty miles by sixty, stretching east from the Big Bend of the Columbia and reaching from Ephrata on the north to the Tri-Cities on the south.

Water stored behind Grand Coulee Dam will eventually fertilize over 1,000,000 acres of high-valued farmland.

AL MONNER

Perhaps man is inspired to such wonders because nature in Washington is not something you put comfortably in the duffel bag of your memory to carry off for another day. The peaks of Rainier and Baker and Shuksan were thought to be gods by the savages, and with reason. The rolling area of a Washington wheat ranch is not perceived in a loving glance, as you might admire an English garden or field of California poppies. The size of the cascade that once poured over the "Dry Falls" of Grand Coulee staggers the imagination; this is the ancient bed of the river and the waterfall

Rolling hills of the Palouse country.

was four miles wide and 100 feet deep, shaking the earth around it for centuries on end.

Yet we do have more modest vistas, and they are, I like to think, as impressive in their way.

I mean some of those jewel-like lakes in the shadow of Rainier; the snow-fed creeks that tumble down from the Olympics and through the bracken toward the Pacific; the Blue Mountains seen through the soft haze of a summer afternoon, shepherding the lovely valley of the Walla Walla.

I mean—say much later that same afternoon, perhaps near to nightfall—the short climb to the knoll from which you can look down on the reconstruction of the Whitman Mission just as it stood until that fearful massacre of 1847. Because, remember, we have history tucked away in our vistas too.

I am thinking of Commencement Bay from the peace of Point Defiance Park in Tacoma. And of Spokane's South Hill, where you step carefully among wild flowers in a mountain meadow, walk beneath tall ponderosa pines—and look far beyond to the rolling hills of the Palouse country. I can never forget a drive I once made through those hills in a gentle rain, and how the gray-white blossoms of the honey locusts drifted down with the rain, perfuming everything. (And should you encounter such a rain in the spring or early summer there, understand that to the wheat and pea and asparagus farmers it is a million-dollar rain. Don't hope aloud that it will clear up!)

I remember a stroll in the green-blue dusk that comes down around Wenatchee, along the river, where the reefer cars of cherries were taking off for Manhattan, far across the continent. And a tiny park in the middle of bustling Olympia with a statue to John Rankin Rogers, author of our "Barefoot School Boy" law.

Be warned that you will not find all of Washington along the main highways. If you are pressed for time, if the fast-paced main trail beckons you inexorably—well, then, you may never know my state as I would like to have you know it.

True, you can go pell-mell south to north, from our Vancouver to the Vancouver of British Columbia, and touch five of Washington's ten largest cities, including the capital. It is true that along this freeway strip live two-thirds of our population. I have known folks who made this journey and claimed to have seen Washington clear.

But where in their diaries is the record of Bremerton, say, with its great Puget Sound naval shipyard geared to a nuclear Navy? Where is Point Roberts, the only American land which can be reached only by sea or through a foreign nation (Canada)? What of the Yakima country, and how about Entiat, the town that had to get up and walk away to higher ground when the Rocky Reach Dam created a lake that covered the old townsite?

You should not miss the ocean beaches, or a long look at Grays Harbor, named for the intrepid merchant skipper who discovered the Columbia, or the communities of Aberdeen and Hoquiam.

You can, if you like, circle the vast Olympic Peninsula in one day. But it has always seemed to me that this is a foolish thing to do, even for those of us who live hereabouts and may go back next month. I would not think of touching the Peninsula without taking that top-of-the-world drive along

Snoqualmie Falls, a 270-foot cataract.

RAY ATKESON

Hurricane Ridge in Olympic National Park.
WASHINGTON DEPT. OF COMMERCE AND ECONOMIC DEVELOPMENT

Hurricane Ridge. From there you can get a new dimension on this strange area. The clouds kiss your forehead and you feel that you might reach out and touch the glaciers.

But, done with such exhilaration, I drop down to quiet Lake Sutherland or Lake Crescent. I stay awhile. I take time enough to drive less than twenty miles along the Hoh until I come to a Forest Guard Station. There, with a little free guidebook in hand, I pursue an easy foot trail into a weird, enchanted world—the rain forest.

Not all the interesting sights are along the highways. The fishing village of Skamokowa nestles in a rocky gap of the Columbia River.   AL MONNER

I saunter the streets of Port Angeles, fresh from celebrating its centennial year. I visit Port Townsend to see again some lovely examples of Victorian architecture, something not easy to find in a state as young as this one.

Or I may go there simply to see how, in the early evening, the sunset paints pink the wings of a soaring gull. Just as sometimes I seek out Whetstone Creek, 300 miles away and across the mountains, because there (at the right time of year) I will see male Chinese pheasants herding their less gaudy mates among the wheat and teaching a tiny brood to "freeze" because the hunter will come.

Those of us who cannot afford Palm Springs or New Mexico know that Washington State has its "sun spots" too. Some are on the Olympic Peninsula, almost unsuspected under the "rain shadows"—curious phenomena of a region celebrated for precipitation. Others are in the eastern part of the state—almost anywhere there, but chiefly in the Soap Lake country, and in the Inland Empire, and near the Idaho border in such communities as Clarkston and Asotin. There are half a dozen others.

Washington has a winter wonderland, too, and that is the land of Hurricane Ridge; of Mount Baker; of Pilchuck; of Glacier Peak, the land of Paradise; and of the passes just east of Yakima and Wenatchee. Loup Loup and Leavenworth and Squilchuck are other magic names in our winter playgrounds.

Almost anywhere you want to go in Washington you'll be reasonably close to an Indian reservation. You'll be welcome and unscalped if you refrain from pidgin English and hunting and fishing. If you cannot get it out of your mind that this is a land of cowboys, you may settle at one of several dude ranches on either side of the Cascade Range and maybe even see some herding and branding in the beef country on the east.

If you are of a philosophical turn, slow down and remember that everywhere in Washington are the scenically big and little, together. I like to lean against a warm dune out on the coast and watch the great Pacific rolling in. Far off is a seiner, moving toward China, slowly sinking behind the horizon, telling me the world is round. As the breakers pound, the sand trembles beneath me, and this is the time, and place, for wonder at the world—and heaven too.

But my smallest daughter has no concern with such matters; nor is she frightened of the sea, or yet of those Army jets marking their trails in vapor far overhead. She finds delight in the tide pools and how she can lean against the wind in a ski-jump stance without falling flat. To her the great Pacific is only another pond's edge for wading, and Olympus only another mountain, no more to be gaped at than Lummi or Mount Si.

I wish you and I could take some of these 60,000 miles of Washington roads as unhurriedly as she explores a beach. But I implore you, if you think you may not return for a time, to plan a wide loop or two within our borders.

The swing around the Olympic Peninsula I have urged already. For a fair idea of the characteristics of both eastern and western Washington, center yourself on Yakima and plan on a drive of 150 miles. You can strike out from Yakima, take one of two mountain passes (Naches or Chi-

Trail near Ohanepecosh Hot Springs in Mt. Rainier National Park. JOHN F. WARTH

nook) to Ohanepecosh in Mount Rainier National Park, skirt the Rimrock and Tieton Dam areas, and return.

If you want to see some Washington dams in addition to Grand Coulee, move out of the Tri-Cities area for McNary Dam, or Ice Harbor Dam on the Snake, or the Lower Monumental on that same tortuous stream.

Or, out of Clarkston, there's a little loop tour that swings through Clarkston Heights and Peola and Pomeroy, returning you to base with a fine conception of the dry-land farming area and Snake River country.

Or just let us know what you expect of Washington. You'll need a bit

McNary Dam on the Columbia generates 1,000,000 kilowatts of electricity.
U. S. CORPS OF ENGINEERS

of local knowledge, so don't hesitate to ask questions. If we look blank, keep on the trail until you reach the next settlement and ask again.

It's all here somewhere, but sometimes some of us forget just where.

The Century 21 "World of Tomorrow" fascinated nearly 10,000,000 visitors and caught the interest of other millions of newspaper readers and television viewers.

The notion of a fair began modestly enough in 1956. The idea was a show to commemorate the fiftieth anniversary of the Alaska-Yukon-Pacific

Exposition, which had begun a new era for the Puget Sound country and the Northwest.

But Washingtonians are never too keen about looking backward. The idea smoldered but did not catch fire. Curiously, the Russians had sown the seed for the old "A-Y-P" Exposition when they practically gave away Alaska for $7,200,000. Ninety years later they fired Sputnik I into orbit and gave Seattle fair enthusiasts a theme. Why should not the new exposition celebrate the Space Age, which ought to be going real good by the dawn of the twenty-first century?

Elsewhere it was intimated that this was a bold fancy for a state so isolated. Seattleites were quick to retort that, after all, the Boeing organization had been assuming a rather remarkable role in the space age. They invited attention to great research projects at the University of Washington and at Washington State University, which was celebrating its liberation from "cow college" status by building a nuclear reactor for peaceful studies.

To the broader point, our more erudite citizens gazed down at the top of a world globe, spun it slowly, and invited attention to a fact not generally understood: in the light of the future—in peace or war—Washington State is not at all isolated. On the contrary, it is central to probable North American and world developments.

But geophysicists and geopoliticians do not build world's fairs. Seattle leaders allowed that they might see their way clear to keep a staff going if $15,000,000 of municipal money could be had for the fair itself. The rest of the state remained unmoved, seeing no generosity in this plan, because the proposed fair would depart, leaving Seattle with a nice new civic center. Other communities were further jaundiced when the state decided to come up with $10,000,000.

The capper arrived when the federal government was persuaded to add $12,000,000 for a Science Pavilion. It was this that inspired a party of Seattleites to jet-line to Paris for the approval of the Bureau of International Expositions.

Gradually, Washingtonians from Blaine on the north to Megler on the south, from Westport on the west to Rosalia on the east, decided that an official World's Fair was indeed just what the doctor recommended for a state that had been a bit uncertain as to how to get from here to the next century. The Alweg people in Sweden saw an opportunity to demonstrate their monorail as a possible cure for U.S. mass-transportation ills. And a group of Seattle capitalists hit upon the idea of a Space Needle restaurant. With those two steps came the symbols needed for world publicity. The Evergreen Land found itself in the limelight, a pleasant and encouraging sensation.

It was so encouraging that nobody blinked when two Japanese architects were handed $350,000 to build an illuminated water fountain. Strangely, there was not even protest that Washington designers could have done it as well and perhaps more cheaply. We had a $100,000,000 fair on our hands. Uncle Sam, the state, Chief Seattle, 26 foreign nations, and more than 100 U.S. companies were involved. It was a thing Washingtonians had to live up to, and they demonstrated their spirit by buying $2,000,000 worth of advance tickets.

But far more than a fair had gripped the imaginations of Washingtonians. The old *Zeitgeist* had returned, the marriage of time and spirit.

This became apparent even before the World's Fair opened its gates on April 21, 1962. When King County Commissioners decided to float a bond issue to buy an expensive "show farm" for a county park, the president of the Citizens Planning Council addressed them in an enthusiastic open letter: "The population projections show that in less than forty years the Puget Sound area will be completely urbanized from the water's edge to the mountains. Future generations will regard this purchase . . . as we now regard the vision of those who in 1856 purchased 840 acres of farm land which later became Manhattan's Central Park."

Here, again, was "New York Alki"—but the "by and by" was closer. In the same week, just seven days before the fair's opening, Seattle's planning director told the public that by 1985 King County would show a population increase equivalent to "another Seattle," by which he meant an additional 600,000 people.

"This means," he said, "240,000 more homes, 267,000 more automobiles, 1700 more miles of roads, 7200 more stores, 158 more schools, and 277,000 more workers." In our World's Fair euphoria we Washingtonians may or may not have received the moral: this growth will be either planned or haphazard.

The picture which this planning director briefly unveiled is not framed only by the borders of Seattle and King County. Well before the actual dawning of the twenty-first century the "strip city" that may be said to begin with Everett on the north and extend to Olympia on the south will hold at least 2,000,000 people.

The trend is not confined to the Puget Sound area. What can happen east of the Cascades is easily seen by the eight-year changes of economic significance in the Columbia Basin reclamation area. Using a comparison region just east of the project, we can note a population increase of nearly 50,000 for the basin against no change for the adjacent area. Industrial establishments increased by 770 in the reclamation acreage and not at all in the area as yet unirrigated. Carloadings increased by 11,000 as against

Cargoes of wheat and fertilizer being towed through McNary Dam.

U. S. CORPS OF ENGINEERS

a decrease of nearly 2000 in the comparison area. The latter, in the eight-year period, showed an increase of 37 per cent in postal receipts and the "new" green land 200 per cent.

The Columbia Basin reclamation story is not yet finished. Possibilities exist for broadening the agricultural base, and as the regional market grows, so will the intensification of the farmers' efforts. Integrated with agricultural growth will be the expanding chemical industries.

In the late fifties and sixties the coming of natural gas by pipeline added a new dimension to the industrial picture in Washington. This

Whitman College at Walla Walla.

important development has not dulled our tremendous appetite for hydro-electric power. Although we lead the nation in both developed and undeveloped water power, nearly all of the economically feasible hydro sites have been exploited. The high cost of construction at less desirable locations may prevent their coming into existence. Or these sites may be made obsolete by new ways of producing electricity.

There are other industries besides aluminum still to be attracted by our low-cost power. Alaska's statehood means increased trade, this time to the advantage of Alaska as well as Puget Sound. Ocean trade with the

Far East must one day return in force, and inexorably on the maritime charts this is still the gateway to the Orient. Already we have a head start in the field of atomic energy. Boeing will build a great share of the huge airliners of tomorrow, help to shoot for the moon, and flirt with Venus too.

We will find ever more uses for wood cellulose and have only begun to discover the value of lignin and other contents of our renewable forests.

But there are other matters in the future of Washington. We are aware that our recreational areas are a resource, too, of a spiritual as well as an economic kind. We understand that there must be social and cultural advances along with the payrolls and the progress.

I can think of no other state in the union which in the next fifty years will offer more excitement or more challenge.

BRITISH COLUMBIA

Roderick Haig-Brown

Mountains dominate a large part of the British Columbia landscape.
Kootenay National Park near Radium.

EASTERN Canadians, prompted by dreams of lotus living, nightmares of unpredictable politics, and a good measure of jealousy, like to refer to British Columbia as the California of Canada. Most British Columbians are willing to take credit for the fact that they are abnormally blessed with superb scenery and temperate climate but suspect that they are inhibited from full enjoyment of either by a puritan tradition somewhat dourly Scottish in origin. Citizens of the eastern United States, if they happen to think of British Columbia at all, probably consider it a good place to go fishing. Westerners, of course, know better, having met there all the disappointments a fisherman should normally expect.

Like Texans, whose state is considerably smaller than the province, British Columbians have never been quite convinced about confederation. They feel it should have gone the other way—that the lesser entity should have joined the greater. As it is, they maintain a healthy suspicion that the man in Ottawa—and, even more certainly, the man in the rest of Ontario—is taking them for a ride. Then, just as the Texan likes to reckon himself a better American than the man in New York or Washington, D.C., the British Columbian is sure he is as good a Canadian as the man in Ottawa, if not better.

Behind these attitudes, which the cheaper politicians play upon so skillfully, there is a shortish history and a lot of geography, most of it mountains.

British Columbia—and the whole Pacific Northwest, for that matter—was a hard place for explorers to reach. Roughly half the world away from Europe, by way of either Cape Horn or the Cape of Good Hope, it was separated from the settled Atlantic Seaboard by the widest part of the continent and the formidable barrier of the Rocky Mountains.

Sir Francis Drake reached northern California and probably beyond in 1578. But two centuries passed before the Spanish, made nervous by British activities in the South Pacific, ventured beyond California toward the rugged, fog-screened northern coastline. Even then their tiny, ill-equipped ships gave them little scope for exploration, and it is probable that Captain James Cook's British expedition of 1776 made the first landing on the coast of what is now British Columbia. Cook's sailors bought sea otter skins from the Indians at Nootka, on the west coast of Vancouver Island, and later sold them at a tremendous profit in China. This brought about the province's first commercial invasion—that of the sea otter traders: Meares, Portlock and Dixon, Gray of the *Columbia*, Captain Barclay of the *Imperial Eagle,* and others left their own names and those of their ships at many places along the broken coastline.

These activities stirred the Spaniards again, and soon an expedition sailed north from San Blas in Mexico to plant the Spanish flag at Nootka and provoke the famous Nootka Incident, which brought Britain and Spain to the edge of war. Diplomacy prevailed in the end, a treaty was signed, and Captain George Vancouver, British Columbia's first real hero, was sent out to settle the matter with the noble Spaniard, Don Quadra, at Nootka. In the course of his mission, Vancouver, a patient and dedicated young seaman, explored and charted every bay and inlet and passage between northern California and northern Alaska with such accuracy that many of his observations hold good today. For the first time the outline of the north-west coastline of North America could be shown on the world's maps in clear detail instead of by cartographers' guesswork.

In 1793, the second summer of Vancouver's great survey, Alexander Mackenzie of the North West Fur Company was coming toward the end of his second great journey across the continent in search of the Western Ocean. His previous effort had taken him to the mouth of the Mackenzie River on the shores of the Arctic Ocean. But this time he pushed forward up the Peace River, passed through its canyons in the Rocky Mountains, turned southward up the Parsnip, and, helped by the Indians, crossed the Arctic divide safely to the still-unnamed Fraser River and the Pacific water-shed. He finally reached salt water near Bella Coola in July, becoming the first man to cross the full width of the continent from ocean to ocean.

Mackenzie showed the way for the overland fur traders, but they were slow to follow it. It was not until twelve years later that Simon Fraser went forward to establish Fort McLeod, the first white settlement in the interior of British Columbia, followed by Fort St. James and Fort Fraser in the following year. In 1805, the year Fraser established Fort McLeod, Lewis and Clark reached the mouth of the Columbia from the eastern United States. Two years later David Thompson, fur trader by vocation, geographer by choice, crossed the Rockies and found the Canadian sources of that great river. In the following year Simon Fraser followed the river of his name out to salt water, to learn in disappointment that it was not the Columbia and that its fearful rapids and canyons offered no satisfactory route for fur traders' business. On his way downstream he named the

Fraser River near Cisco.   B. C. GOVERNMENT PHOTO

Thompson River, which joins the Fraser from the east at Lytton, in the mistaken thought "that David Thompson and our friends from Fort des Prairies may be encamped at the source of it."

From this stage the North West Company began to build everything from the Columbia River north into a solid fur traders' empire. In 1813 the company bought out Fort Astoria, the American post at the mouth of the Columbia. At the same time, John Stuart, Fraser's second-in-command, traveled overland from the Fraser to Okanagan Lake and found a pack-horse route to the Columbia. Posts were quickly established at Walla Walla,

Alexandria, and Okanogan; Astoria was renamed Fort George and soon became the luxurious capital of the empire, supplied by ships sailing round Cape Horn from Europe and the Eastern Seaboard.

By 1821 the North West Company, in spite of its strength and aggressiveness, was finding the Pacific Northwest, with its extended lines of communication, a little too much to handle. The wintering partners swallowed their pride and joined with the Hudson's Bay Company. In 1824 the great Dr. McLoughlin, a former North Wester, was sent to take charge at Fort George. He soon moved the post to Fort Vancouver and developed extensive farmlands, a sawmilling operation, and the beginnings of an export trade in fish and lumber, in addition to the fur trade. For the next ten or fifteen years all went smoothly and the company steadily increased its hold on the land, developing farms at Nisqually on Puget Sound and in the Cowlitz Valley, as well as at Fort Vancouver, Walla Walla, and Fort Colville. It entered formidably into the coastal trade with six sailing vessels and the *Beaver,* the first steamship on the Pacific Coast, and steadily improved communications by the brigade trails with Kamloops and Alexandria and Fort St. James in the north. It seemed reasonable to believe that the company was securely and permanently established from the Columbia northward, and Dr. McLoughlin did so believe.

Governor George Simpson, the head of the company, was far less certain. Between great canoe journeys that took him across the continent to visit New Caledonia and the Columbia Department, Simpson journeyed frequently to the great worlds of New York and London. By 1835 or earlier he had begun to suspect that United States pressure would sooner or later make it difficult to hold on south of the forty-ninth parallel without powerful British help, which seemed unlikely to be forthcoming. In 1837 Captain McNeill of the SS *Beaver* made a first report on the present site of the city of Victoria. In 1842 Chief Factor James Douglas was sent to make a further report, and in the following year he returned to establish Fort Victoria.

The site chosen, at the southern tip of Vancouver Island, reflected Simpson's determination that if the boundary should finally be set at the forty-ninth parallel, at least he would hold the whole of Vancouver Island. Three years later, on June 15, 1846, the Oregon Boundary Treaty settled on the forty-ninth parallel but accepted a southward dip through the San Juan Islands, to leave the whole of Vancouver Island and half the width of the Strait of Juan de Fuca in British hands. Within four or five years Fort Victoria on Camosun Inlet replaced Fort Vancouver on the Columbia as the headquarters of the company's interests west of the Rockies.

Bastion at Nanaimo on Vancouver Island was built by the Hudson's Bay Company.
B. C. GOVERNMENT PHOTO

James Douglas, who had been an eighteen-year-old clerk in the North West Company at the time of the union with the Hudson's Bay Company, took charge of the company's affairs in the newly defined land. He was a tall, handsome, weather-beaten man in his forties, strong-willed and thoroughly experienced. He was to become, in a very real and lively sense, the founder of British Columbia.

British Columbia did not come into being all at once. The mainland area remained a fur traders' preserve, remote and difficult behind its guardian mountain ranges. Vancouver Island became a colony under the British Crown and Douglas its governor. The company received important concessions and in return was supposed to promote settlement. In fact, it discouraged settlers in just about every way it could and did its best to maintain the colony also as a private reserve. A few settlers clustered around Sooke, forced out there by the high land prices nearer Victoria. The company itself established four large farms at Craigflower, Colwood, View-field, and Constance Cove, which bailiffs ran like country estates, and a few more settlers arrived. Coal was discovered in good quantity at Nanaimo, after abortive efforts to develop mines farther north, and in 1854, the *Princess Royal* brought a number of Staffordshire miners with their families. James Douglas struggled with all the unfamiliar problems of government, building schools, setting up courts, holding an election on the orders of the Colonial Office, encouraging the export of lumber, fish, and coal.

If economic progress was slow, life was gay in the young colony, especially when the Royal Navy ships put in and their officers came ashore. Then the governor put on his fine uniform, salutes were fired, and calls were made and returned; there were balls, picnics, hunting parties, horse races. These were the times that formed Victoria's character as a Navy town and a capital city, and their influence holds to this day.

But the quiet times were almost over. Gold was being reported in increasing quantities from the Thompson River. The wary Hudson's Bay men kept it as quiet as possible and did little to encourage the Indians in their discoveries. But gold, as Douglas well knew, cannot be kept quiet. In California thousands of miners and prospectors, left high and dry by the aftermath of the '49 rush, were awaiting just such a call. In March of 1858 the advance guard arrived, a small group of miners who crossed to the Fraser from Victoria and found gold at Hill's Bar, just above Fort Hope. By midsummer little Fort Victoria was surrounded by a sea of white tents and temporary buildings housing some 20,000 people. The miners worked their way steadily on from there, across the Gulf, up the Fraser, to Spuzzum and Boston Bar, to Lytton, Lillooet, Bridge River, and Big Bar, finding gold all the way.

Every race and creed and color, every kind of man, good and bad, honest and dishonest, tough and mild, brutal and kindly, was represented in this first great rush: "The most clamorous," someone said, "and politically speaking the most unreasonable people in the world." But somehow James Douglas kept them in order, supplied their needs, gave them law, smoothed out their troubles with the Indian peoples. All the while he was in close communication with the Colonial Office in London. At first he governed by improvisation and by the force of his own personality. But toward the end of the year help arrived in the form of a company of Royal Engineers under Col. Moody and a magnificent, bearded, sharp-eyed judge, Matthew Baillie Begbie. At Fort Langley, on November 19, 1858, the mainland was formally declared the colony of British Columbia and James Douglas was sworn in as its first governor.

The search for gold lasted several years, leading men on up the Fraser, across the interior plateau, and into the Cariboo Mountains, where the gold was coarser and richer but deeper and harder to realize. Barkerville, some sixty miles east of Quesnel, with rich diggings on Williams Creek, was the peak of the excitement and in the early sixties was said to be the largest settlement on the continent west of Chicago. The miners went beyond there into the Omineca Mountains and over to the Arctic watershed, but no comparable finds were made and the Cariboo country, producing several million dollars in gold a year, remained the treasure house of the new colony. With the help of Moody's Engineers, Douglas built a road through the Fraser Canyons; the Cariboo road reached on from there to the mines, with its pack trains and wagon trains, its stagecoaches and closely guarded gold expresses. At one time there was a camel caravan that frightened everything else off the roads and led to a flock of damage suits; at another time a fleet of steam-driven traction engines bogged down in the mud. Incredibly venturesome river-boat captains took their stern-wheelers and side-wheelers as far up the river as Fort George.

There were late-comers—the Overlanders of '62, struggling across northern Ontario and the prairies from comfortable eastern settlements; men coming from Britain by way of the Australian gold rush; others from here, there, and everywhere, who arrived through immense hardships, bedraggled and broke, to find that the fine flush of gold seeking was over. Being the men and women they were, they turned to honest settlement, to agriculture, to trade, to the first struggle to realize wealth from the great coastal forests and the immense abundance of the salmon fisheries.

It is hard to write of these people without a sense of nostalgia for the grandeur and courage of the past. The Comox settlers of 1862, who ventured northward on Vancouver Island to take over a land "undisturbed by aught but the howl of the wild beasts or the formal tread of the deer and elk"; the Overlanders and others like them, who turned to work on the roads, in the mines, in sawmill and shingle mill, and who founded the city of Vancouver and rebuilt it as an act of faith after the cataclysmic fire of 1886; still others, who went to grow grain at Salmon Arm and Enderby; young Englishmen who came to make fruit farms and a good life in the Okanagan and Thompson valleys; the men who carried cattle ranches northward from Osoyoos by Penticton to Kamloops and the Cariboo —all these set the tone and pace of the country, contributing judges and magistrates and civil servants, engineers and dreamers and eccentrics, until the start of the First World War. Time has tempered their influence upon the country since then, but much of it remains to make British Columbia a different and better place.

Through the acute stage of the gold rush, James Douglas continued as governor of the two colonies—Vancouver Island and British Columbia. He retired in 1864, and two years later the two colonies were united, with much debate and politicking as to whether the capital of the united colonies should be at Victoria or at New Westminster. The Victoria faction finally prevailed by getting the leading orator of the other side gloriously drunk and scrambling his notes so effectively that he repeated the opening lines of his speech half a dozen times and sat down with only a vague sense that things were not entirely right. Worse decisions have certainly been made on far better grounds.

In 1871 the colony joined the Dominion of Canada and became the Province of British Columbia. A railroad was one of the promises of confederation, but it had to cross the wastes of northern Ontario, the width of the prairies, the Rocky Mountains, the Selkirks, and Monashee range and then follow the Thompson River and pass through the canyons of the Fraser to reach tidewater, so it was not completed until 1886.

In spite of the brave sounds British Columbia made at the time of confederation, her population, apart from some 35,000 native Indians, numbered only 15,000. Among these were the fur traders and coal miners and a few agricultural settlers, but the great majority were those who had followed the gold rushes and stayed on. Confederation brought a slow increase to 25,000 in the following decade, and the railroad tripled that to 75,000 by 1891. At the turn of the century, with the development of the Okanagan fruit lands and the Kootenay base-metal mines and the steady growth of the logging industry, British Columbia had become a land of excitement and opportunity, with a population of over 150,000 that was steadily growing. Most of the immigrants were from the British Isles or eastern Canada, but Scandinavians were coming to the logging areas and other European countries were becoming aware of the lively possibilities of the mountainous province at the edge of the Pacific.

In some ways these years before the First War were the golden years of settlement. British Columbia was supremely the land of opportunity for the independent mind, the small man who wanted to be his own master. A house and a few acres of land were within the reach of almost anyone. Seasonal work in the mines, in the woods, in the fisheries yielded a cash income for clearing and development. The joys of outdoor life, hunting, fishing, and unspoiled country were open to anyone who cared to reach for them. The ambitious could get a start on limited capital as small logging operators, orchardists, cattle ranchers, road contractors; they could prospect the hills in search of new mines, stake timber in the great coastal forests, and find footholds in the growing salmon industry.

Men who responded to such challenges as these were only too prompt to answer the call of World War I. Settlements like Duncan on Vancouver Island and Wallachin in the Thompson Valley sent every able-bodied man. Volunteers flocked in from the Okanagan farms and the Kootenay mines, from Cariboo cattle ranches and coastal inlets, from faraway points in the Omineca Mountains and the northern valleys. Many came back when the war was over, but many did not. Many of the old patterns of life went on, but in subtle ways they were changing or had already changed. Steam had come to the woods in the early part of the century. By the start of the twenties, great companies were pushing railroad operations far back from salt water. Overfishing and disastrous slides in the Fraser Canyons had reduced the Fraser salmon runs and made it clear that salmon was not an inexhaustible resource. Vancouver was growing into a big city, though not quite so big as the real-estate speculators hoped. Land was still to be had and settlers still came to it; life was still free and good for the independent spirit, but perhaps not quite so free as it once had been.

Even in the depression years, British Columbia attracted settlers. It was an easier climate to be broke in than many of the others: a rowboat and a hand line would still catch salmon and earn a dollar or two; there were logs on the beaches for fuel and deer in the woods for meat. Country people, especially on the coast, made out fairly well in the depression, yet those years—perhaps even more than the years after the Second World War—seemed to signal the change to urbanization and industrialization. In the province's 1961 population of over 1,500,000, only 13 per cent of the people were directly involved in the great primary industries—logging, mining, fishing, and agriculture. Some 15 per cent were dependent on the manufacturing industries and over 70 per cent were in the service industries. This reflects the increased efficiency of primary production that has occurred all over the continent, releasing more and more people to the service industries. On the surface, it suggests that the province is no longer in a pioneering state. But it is important to remember that three-quarters of the province's population is concentrated down in the southwest corner, around Vancouver and Victoria, leaving 300,000 square miles of country to the rest. There are still homesteads to be settled, valleys to be explored, mountains to be prospected—and people are doing all these things.

The gold rush brought men of every kind and creed and color. The years that followed brought mainly British and Scandinavians, with some Chinese and Japanese. (It has been said that the Canadian Pacific right-of-way was blasted through the Fraser canyons and the Selkirk range by Chinese and young Englishmen.) In spite of extensive immigration in the years since World War II, three-quarters of the people of the province are now Canadian-born: about two-thirds are of British origin, with Scandinavians, Germans, French, Dutch, and native Indians following, in that order. No other group is represented by more than 2 per cent of the population.

The native Indians of British Columbia were probably the wealthiest, most highly developed, and most secure people on the continent before the coming of the Europeans. It is believed that there were at least 75,000 of them in the late eighteenth century in half a dozen great language groups and so well spread through the length and breadth of the province that an account of them describes much of the area's geography.

The wealth of the Indian peoples was chiefly in the sea and the salmon runs, so the coastal groups were generally the most advanced. The Nootkas of the west coast of Vancouver Island and their Makah relatives on the southern end of the island and the northern point of the Olympic Peninsula were hunters of sea mammals—whales, seals, sea lions, sea otters—and it was Captain Cook's meeting with them at Friendly Cove that led to the development of the sea otter trade. Captain Vancouver, passing through the Strait of Juan de Fuca, met with tribes of the great Coast Salish group in Puget Sound, the Gulf Islands, and the Strait of Georgia. In spite of some misunderstandings and warlike gestures at the head of Puget Sound—near the present site of Olympia, Washington—he found them generally a helpful and friendly people and was especially well received by the Capilano band, whose descendants still live just across Burrard Inlet from the city of Vancouver, at the approaches to the Lion's Gate Bridge. Still another group of Salish people helped the

Hell's Gate fishways, on Fraser River, rescued salmon runs valued at many millions of dollars. B. C. GOVERNMENT PHOTO

expedition's boats through the difficult Arran Rapids at the mouth of Bute Inlet. North of Bute Inlet the expedition passed into the territory of the Kwakiutls, a more aggressive and socially organized people, who also proved friendly and helpful. The Kwakiutls were, and are, superb carvers, skillful fishermen, and great composers of songs and dances.

In the second summer of his exploration, Vancouver reached the Bella Coolas, a group of Interior Salish people who had found their way to the coast and become almost indistinguishable from the Kwakiutls, though he noticed their skill in weaving and the beauty of their goat-hair blankets.

North of Kwakiutl territory, which probably ended just beyond Milbank Sound, he was among the Tsimshians—another great salmon people—who were carvers of totem poles, clever designers, and able organizers. Across Hecate Strait, the Queen Charlotte Islands are Haida territory. Like the Nootkas, the Haidas were wonderful canoe makers and splendid seamen —crab and halibut fishermen and hunters of sea mammals. Unlike the Nootkas, they did not hunt whales but increased their wealth by sending out raiding parties in great war canoes that traveled as far south as the mouth of the Columbia, surprising and terrorizing other tribes along the way. They also were totem-pole people, carvers of great skill and originality.

Just above the northern boundary of the province, in what are now southern Alaskan waters, are the Tlingits, possibly the most sophisticated and certainly the most aggressive of the coastal tribes. Here for the first time, Vancouver's expedition met with hostility that could not be appeased and determined attacks that wounded some of the seamen. Vancouver and his officers admired the great chiefs in their beautifully designed Chilcat blankets and ermine-fringed headdresses but never dared trust them far.

The sea and salmon wealth of these coastal tribes left them free to develop arts and evolve social philosophies and organizations that are only becoming fully understood today. White civilization attacked their beliefs and brought diseases—smallpox, influenza, measles, and others—which reduced the Indians' numbers to less than a third and destroyed the leadership and organization of the tribes. But the people have survived and have been increasing rapidly over the past thirty years. Many are skillful and success-ful fishermen, using modern methods and equipment. Most of the ancient arts have been preserved in some degree and adapted to modern uses: the Cowichan Indian sweaters reflect the weaving skills of the Salish people; the argillite-slate carvings and silverwork of the Haidas still express the people's wonderful understanding of design; and some of the Kwakiutl wood carvers are reproducing the arts of their fathers with a sureness and feeling that command respect. It is not at all difficult to imagine that these qualities may flower again into major artistic achievements within the next few decades.

The land explorers found simpler and shier peoples in the interior of the province. Coming up the Peace and Parsnip rivers, Mackenzie was among the Beaver and Sekani tribes of the great Athapascan language group, wandering hunters who showed themselves seldom and reluctantly. Crossing the divide to the Fraser watershed, he came into the territory of the Carrier tribe, which later supported the posts at Fort McLeod, Fort St. James, and Fort George by bringing in furs. The Indians who warned him of the dangers of the river below Quesnel and guided him

Indian village near Hazelton.   B. C. GOVERNMENT PHOTO

along the West Road River toward the coastal divide were still Carriers, though of different bands. He reached salt water in Bella Coola territory and found the Indians there the finest canoemen he had ever seen.

Simon Fraser did not turn back at the Quesnel but held on downriver. So he came into the territory of the Interior Salish, salmon people again but upriver people who took their toll from the runs by spear and net and trap as they passed. At the junction of the Fraser and the Thompson, near the present site of Lytton, he came upon a great gathering of tribes—Shuswaps, Thompsons, Lillooets, and Nicolas—where he was splendidly entertained by many great chiefs and great orators. They passed him on downriver to other bands, which helped him over the precipitous trails along the rock walls of the canyons until he came to the lower river and the Coast Salish.

David Thompson crossed the Rockies into the territory of the Kootenays, a people he quickly learned to love. They were bold and warlike, yet trustworthy and honorable. "They pride themselves on their industry and skill in doing anything," he wrote. "They are as neat and cleanly in their persons as circumstances will allow. I found them a fine race of moral Indians, the finest I have seen." The Kootenay Indians at that time probably numbered barely 1000 all told. Yet one of their chiefs had led a war party over 1000 miles to the south and had successfully raided a Spanish silver train; the Indians had the horses and packsaddles as proof of their deed, though they had discarded the useless white metal.

None of these Indian peoples was conquered and no Indian wars were fought. A punitive expedition was sent into the Chilcotin after the massacre of two small parties which were starting a road from the head of Bute Inlet in 1864, and naval ships occasionally shelled one or another of the coastal villages when there were difficulties between Indians and settlers, but generally the Indians accepted and welcomed the settlers and the early settlers found the Indians helpful and useful. Dr. Margaret Ormsby noted in her *British Columbia: A History* that both James Douglas and Judge Begbie "had a sensitive regard for the welfare of the Native Indian." Others who came later were less understanding and less considerate, and the toll of the exotic diseases was far more terrible than war. But it is becoming clear at last that the Northwest Indians have a major part to play in the lands they once owned.

British Columbia is so vast that generalizations are bound to be unsatisfactory. In popular conception, it is a damp and rainy place of mild and gentle climate. This is scarcely true, even on the Pacific Coast, where the city of Victoria has a rainfall of less than 30 inches and an annual average of well over 2000 hours of sunshine, while winter temperatures at the heads of the long inlets frequently drop well below zero and the Vancouver Island mountains carry 25 to 40 feet of snow each winter. Henderson Lake on the west coast of Vancouver Island has an annual rainfall of more than 250 inches, while the Thompson River Valley in the interior of the province has less than seven. In Vancouver and Victoria roses may bloom at Christmas time, albeit somewhat sadly, while Smith River in the northern part of the province, has known 74 below zero.

British Columbians like to remind themselves that Prince George, 500

In this area explorer David Thompson found the Kootenays, a people he quickly learned to love.   B. C. GOVERNMENT PHOTO

miles from Vancouver by road, is still less than halfway up the province. They remember that when all the islands are counted and the length of the great inlets is added up, they have over 7000 miles of coastline. The province has literally thousands of fresh-water lakes, both large and small, and a score of mountain ranges, any one of which would be a major feature in most countries. It is, in fact, a very large and complex land area which can reproduce almost any climate found in the northern temperate zones and a number of those found in the Arctic and subArctic.

Because of this diversity, British Columbians are inclined to think of

Cariboo Highway traverses undulating, peaceful farm and ranch country.

B. C. GOVERNMENT PHOTO

their province in terms of regions, most of which are valleys between high mountain ranges. In the south there is the west coast of Vancouver Island, which takes most of its climate directly from the Pacific Ocean and so is generally mild and wet, and the Gulf of Georgia, which roughly includes the east coast of Vancouver Island and the Lower Mainland, including Vancouver and the Fraser Valley as far as Hope. Beyond Hope there is a 100-mile wide intrusion of the Cascade Range from Washington and the Hope-Princeton Highway passes through Manning Park in the heart of the range, then drops down beyond Penticton to the fruitgrowing Okanagan

Valley, which has a mild and gentle climate, with warm summers and little rainfall. Beyond the Okanagan is the West Kootenay, across the Monashee Mountains, and finally the East Kootenay, along the trench between the Selkirks and the Rockies. Each of these regions has its own climate and characteristics and, it is not too much to say, its own way of life.

North of Vancouver Island is Queen Charlotte Sound, which, like the west coast of the island, gets its weather directly from the Pacific; and beyond the sound are the Queen Charlotte Islands, with a rainfall that varies from heavy to moderate. Generally the whole mainland coast northward from Smith Sound to Prince Rupert is a high-rainfall area, with precipitation of 100 inches or more. But once the peaks of the Coast Range are passed and the land eases off to the great interior plateau, the climate is dry again.

The interior plateau, which is rolling hills rather than flatland, is the true heart of the province. It extends from Osoyoos at the border; spreads northward past Merritt to take in the Thompson Valley, the Chilcotin, and the Cariboo; and continues northward beyond Prince George to Finlay Forks and the start of the Omineca Mountains. Beyond these it becomes the Stikine Plateau, which extends to the Yukon Border between the Coast Range and the Cassiar. East of Finlay Forks, across the Rocky Mountains, lies the Peace River country, and to the northward is the Nelson River Basin.

In a country so vast and mountainous, with a population that is still only slightly in excess of 1,600,000, it is easy to understand that transportation and communications have always been problems. Yet main highways are good throughout most of the southern half of the province and a determined traveler can find his way to almost anywhere except the peaks of the mountains by logging roads, ranch roads, mining roads, and pipeline or power-line trails—though it is as well not to venture too far off the public roads without some sort of local advice or guidance. Some of the public roads, such as the Big Bend Highway around the Columbia River's great northward loop, the North Thompson road to Yellowhead Pass, and the Chilcotin road to Bella Coola should not be approached without considerable respect and an extra spare tire or two.

Two transcontinental railroads cross the province. The Canadian Pacific enters by Banff and the Crowsnest Pass in the Rockies and crosses the Selkirks and Monashees by way of Golden, Revelstoke, and Kamloops to follow the Thompson and the Fraser to Vancouver; the Canadian National enters by Jasper and Yellowhead Pass, follows the North Thompson to Kamloops, and then takes the same way as the C.P.R. along the Thompson and

Development of Peace River canyon will eventually add millions of kilowatts to the Pacific Northwest's power supply. B. C. GOVERNMENT PHOTO

*Twisting and turning along the mountains, the Canadian Pacific Railroad emphasizes
the struggle to unlock the province's rich natural resources.*

the Fraser to Vancouver. A second branch follows the upper Fraser to Prince George and continues westward by way of the Bulkley and Skeena Rivers to Prince Rupert, the province's major northern port.

A third railroad, the Pacific Great Eastern, is rather unhappily owned by the good people of the province. Its southern terminus is North Vancouver, across Burrard Inlet from Vancouver itself. From there it follows round the shore of Howe Sound to Squamish, then through the Coast Range to reach the interior plateau at Lillooet, the old starting point of the Cariboo Highway. Beyond Lillooet it is in the rolling Cariboo range country and passes through Williams Lake to Prince George. A recent extension crosses the Arctic divide near Fort McLeod, follows the Parsnip, then cuts through the Rockies by Pine Pass to serve Dawson Creek and Fort St. John in the Peace River country. The P.G.E. has some spectacular scenery and, though passengers are treated somewhat worse than cattle, a trip in its diesel-driven Budd cars, close relatives to streetcars, is well worth while because it is the cheapest and easiest way into many parts of the province not easily seen otherwise. The economics of the P.G.E. have long been and still are somewhat peculiar and quite distressing to its owners, the public. But it may well have a future. The immense discoveries of oil and natural gas in the Peace River country, the increasing northern timber cut, and the probable establishment of pulp mills beyond Prince George suggest that it will one day pay its way.

Travel along the wonderful mountainous coastline of the province has been changing steadily over the past thirty years. A continuous coastal road from Vancouver north to Prince Rupert remains a practical impossibility, in spite of modern road-building methods and machinery. The Coast Mountains come right to the sea's edge. The shore line is often precipitous, nearly everywhere rocky. A coastal road would have to skirt the edges of the inlets, some of them nearly 100 miles long, or else bridge them one by one.

As settlement developed in the late nineteenth and early twentieth centuries, a truly great coastal steamship service built up, following and improving upon traditions set by old Hudson's Bay ships like the *Beaver*. Canadian National, Canadian Pacific, and Union Steamships all contributed to the service, the last two poking their way into tiny bays and coves, up to the heads of the long inlets, anywhere and everywhere that settlement offered business or needed service, calling at isolated logging camps and fishing camps, canneries and sawmills, mine and ranch and Indian settlements. They were elegant ships with comfortable staterooms, first-class dining rooms, promenade decks—deep-sea liners on a small scale; their captains handled them with boldness and certainty in the narrow waters, through

Beach at Tlell on lonely Queen Charlotte Islands.   B. C. GOVERNMENT PHOTO

fog and snowstorm and gale, bringing mail and freight and passengers and the reminder that the great world was still going on outside. *Adelaide, Maquinna, Cardena, Catala, Venture, Chelhosin*—no one who lived upcoast a few years back is likely to forget those steamer names or to remember them without a sense of friendliness and gratitude.

Change has been rapid since World War II. Floatplanes with pilots as dedicated as the old skippers now duck into the little out-of-the-way logging camps and settlements to save the lives of sick and injured people, bring in the spare part that is holding up the job, or just to supply fresh milk and

On Vancouver Island a surfaced highway runs 175 miles from Victoria to Campbell River.   B. C. GOVERNMENT PHOTO

vegetables where such things were once rare luxuries. Smaller motor vessels carry freight and passengers on shorter runs and, very gradually, ferry links across the inlets and from island to island are extending road travel and making the old dream of a coastal highway from Vancouver to Prince Rupert—even though a somewhat broken one—something more than a visionary concept.

Within the past fifteen years the province has developed what might be called a skeleton system of black-topped highways that follow most of the main routes. On Vancouver Island, well served by ferry services from

Vancouver to Victoria and Nanaimo, a surfaced highway runs 175 miles from Victoria to Campbell River and will shortly hold on to Kelsey Bay on Johnstone Strait. A hard-surfaced branch turns off past Mount Arrowsmith to Port Alberni at the head of Alberni Inlet on the west coast. From Vancouver the Trans-Canada Highway runs eastward to Hope, then northward through the Fraser Canyon to turn eastward again at Cache Creek, along the Thompson by Kamloops, and through the Monashee Range to Revelstoke. There it loses itself in gravel and potholes around the Big Bend of the Columbia, soon perhaps to be drowned in the flooding behind Mica Creek Dam. But a new link from Revelstoke in a straight line across the Selkirk Mountains through Rogers Pass to Golden was opened in 1962; it reveals a whole new world of superb mountain scenery that the traveler has seen until now only from the windows of the railroad observation cars. The new link also opens an easier way to the Banff-Windermere Highway and the glories of the Columbia ice fields.

A second main road serving the south of the province branches off at Hope to Princeton and Keremeos and then follows just above the border to the great mining and smelting center of Trail. A little beyond Trail it is turned northward by rough country to Kootenay Lake and the East Kootenays, but here too a mountain link should be completed quite soon. From Cache Creek, where the Trans-Canada Highway turns up the Thompson River, a good road runs northward to join the old Cariboo Highway, now smoothly black at Clinton, and on by Williams Lake and Quesnel to Prince George. Westward from Prince George the road passes through Vanderhoof, Fort Fraser, Hazelton, and Terrace to Prince Rupert. Northward, it crosses the Arctic divide to McLeod Lake and swings eastward through Pine Pass to the Peace River, where it joins the Alaska Highway.

These main highways, twisting and turning along their narrow valleys between the mountains, sharing the canyons with the railroads, struggling over the mountain passes, are themselves spectacular and satisfying routes of travel. They dramatize the province's difficulties by their own, emphasizing the struggle that has gone on from the earliest days to provide transportation that will unlock the resources of mine, field, and forest. They suggest, too, the strength of the province's future. If these are the main routes—following, as they do for the most part, ways originally found by explorers and fur traders and early surveyors 100 years or more ago—how much more difficult must the more remote ways be? And how much in unrealized wealth does their difficulty represent? Unquestionably, the total is large. And just as certainly the steady technological progress of the twentieth century tends always to open new ways and provide access where it was once an economic, if not a physical, impossibility.

Boom of logs on the Fraser River at New Westminster.   WILLIAMS BROS.

British Columbia's greatest resource is in her forests. She shared with Washington and Oregon the superb sawmill timber of the Pacific Northwest—Douglas fir, western hemlock, and red cedar on Vancouver Island and the lower mainland—and on this much of her early economy was built. The best of the sawmill timber has now been stripped away, and much of the forest yield must be realized through pulp mills and plywood plants, but it remains true that some forty cents of every dollar earned in the province comes from the forests.

About 60 per cent of the province's area is in commercial forest, with a theoretical potential yield of some 3,000,000,000 cubic feet a year. In fact, the annual cut is a little over 1,000,000,000 cubic feet, and even this is realized only by putting an excessive strain on the more accessible coastal forests, which have borne the burden of heavy cutting for over half a century. The greater share of the cut is gradually shifting to the smaller and sparser timber of the interior forests, a trend which will continue and which should increase the annual cut to about 1,750,000,000 feet by 1975. But any hope of realizing the full potential of the forests remains in the far more distant future, since a high proportion of the stands are economically inaccessible or else of a size and type that cannot find a place in present world markets.

These few bald figures give some idea of the size and importance of the province's forest industry and a suggestion of its future. But the immensity and variety of the forests is far from clear in them. While it is true that the great Douglas fir stands of the lower mainland and the east coast of Vancouver Island are a thing of the past, tremendous stands of cedar and hemlock and true fir still cover the western slopes of Vancouver Island and the Coast Range. In the Queen Charlotte Islands there is more hemlock and some of the finest Sitka spruce in the world—huge trees, 6 to 12 feet at the butt and 200 or 300 feet high, whose light, tough wood supplied the aircraft industry of two world wars.

In the interior are stands of Douglas fir, hemlock, yellow pine, cedar, lodgepole pine, larch, and cottonwood. In the far north are more spruce and more pine. And in the future there will be pulp mills and more pulp mills, plywood plants, specialized sawmills, and probably plants for chemical and synthetic uses of wood only dreamed of today.

Less than thirty years ago most logging camps were rough and remote collections of shops, bunkhouses, and a cookhouse—the haunts of single men with few responsibilities. Today many are within commuting distance of small towns and cities or are small cities in their own right, with family houses, schools, and community centers. The logger, who is the country's symbol and a part of its true aristocracy, has come into his own as community man and family man. His tools now are rubber-tired and diesel-driven —instead of steel-tired and steam-driven—and huge, powerful, and ever more complicated. His skills, as they always were, are in the moving of massive logs swiftly, economically, and safely to a place of manufacture.

The place of manufacture is no longer a simple sawmill that cuts lumber and burns everything that cannot be made into lumber. It is a giant plant, carefully calculated to make the fullest possible use of every log. It includes a sawmill, a plywood plant, a sulphite pulp mill to turn out newsprint, and

The big log raft heads for the lumber mill.   WILLIAMS BROS.

a sulphate pulp mill to turn out kraft pulp for cartons and kraft paper. Altogether, it is a complex of manufacturing that can support a small city and all its services. The main pulp mills of the province are at Port Alberni, Port Alice, Duncan Bay, Harmac, and Crofton on Vancouver Island; at New Westminster, Woodfibre, Powell River, and Ocean Falls along the mainland coast; at Port Edward near Prince Rupert; and at Castlegar in the Kootenays. Within the next few years many of these plants will be enlarged and new ones will certainly be built, especially in the northern interior.

THE ROSSLAND MINES

You have entered the crater of an ancient volcano rich in minerals. The waste dumps are the remains of famous Rossland mines staked in 1890 by prospectors passing on the near-by Dewdney Trail. From these fabulously rich workings came 6,000,000 tons of ore worth $125,000,000. The City of Rossland and the huge smelter at Trail were born of these mines.

DEPARTMENT OF
RECREATION & CONSERVATION

B. C. GOVERNMENT PHOTO

From the earliest days of coal and gold, mining has always been a major activity in the province; in the past 100 years some $4,000,000,000 worth of minerals has been produced. Coal, which founded the towns of Ladysmith, Nanaimo, Union Bay, and Cumberland on Vancouver Island and Michel and Fernie in the East Kootenays, is no longer being mined to any extent, though large reserves exist in many parts of the province and may one day be economically valuable again. Gold has accounted for some $500,000,000 of the province's mineral yield. The present fixed price discourages mining, and the Bralorne Mine at Bridge River is now the only major producer,

Smelter at Trail is a mighty economic factor in the Kootenays.

B. C. GOVERNMENT PHOTO

though an upward revaluation would bring other mines back into production and might even stimulate the development of new mines.

Copper, like gold, has yielded about $500,000,000. The Britannia Mine on Howe Sound, just north of Vancouver, has long been the major copper producer of western Canada, and Copper Mountain near Princeton, Anyox near Prince Rupert, and the Granby Mine at Phoenix are among great producers of the past. There are many copper properties in various parts of the province, one or two of them highly promising, and it is by no means unlikely that another major producer remains to be found somewhere in the unexplored immensity of the Coast Range.

The most important mines in the province are the silver-lead-zinc properties of the southeast, and, of them all, the Sullivan Mine at Kimberley, discovered in 1892, is by far the greatest. Altogether, these mines have yielded nearly $2,500,000,000—90 per cent of the lead, 50 per cent of the zinc, and 50 per cent of the silver mined in the whole of Canada. The Sullivan Mine largely supports the great Consolidated Mining and Smelting works at Trail and is a mighty factor in the prosperity of the Kootenays. Mining excitements, large and small, are a part of the life of British Columbia and probably always will be. Most British Columbians buy at least a few mining shares sooner or later and many play the penny stocks as faithfully as Britishers play the football pools. A few of the less successful among us may be forgiven if we wonder whether more money goes into the ground than ever comes out of it, but there is always a new crop of investors to replace such cynics.

One postwar development of significance is the mining of iron ore for export, mainly to Japan. Another is the discovery of high-grade asbestos in the Cassiar Mountains. Most of the iron deposits are small but lend themselves quite well to concentration and, when near tidewater, can be profitably worked. This activity has stimulated search, and it is now believed that there are sufficient reserves to warrant the establishment of a steel mill when the local market expands to justify it. The Cassiar Asbestos Mine on the Liard watershed, some 60 miles from the Yukon boundary, has justified development in spite of its remoteness and now produces over 30,000 tons a year, worth about $10,000,000.

British Columbians, the boosters and politicians among them especially, love to talk largely of the vast mineral wealth of the province and of fabulous discoveries yet to be made. Mining men intensely dislike such talk. They wisely point out that much of the province has already been closely prospected and that discovery of new ore bodies, if they exist at all, will always be slow, costly, and difficult. But there is not much doubt that the optimism of ordinary British Columbians will long survive such

Apples are a major crop in the Okanagan Valley.   B. C. GOVERNMENT PHOTO

warnings or that mining excitements will continue to brighten the life of
the province until the last rock has been drilled.

The most productive agricultural land in the province is in the Lower
Fraser Valley, the delta lands that extend from a little below Hope to the
mouth of the river. Most of this land has to be diked against the river's
floods, but it makes splendid pasture and silage and produces about two-
thirds of the total dairy yield, as well as valuable crops of vegetables and
small fruits. The Peace River country is excellent northern-prairie wheat-
land, with some 2,000,000 acres still undeveloped. The Okanagan Valley,

Wheat in the Peace River country.　　　　　　　　　　WILLIAMS BROS.

much of which is irrigated, produces great crops of apples, pears, plums, peaches, and apricots, as well as some dairy products, beef, vegetables, and grain. Because of its ideal climate and living conditions, it was settled early and is now one of the most prosperous and delightful parts of the province.

The Kamloops and Cariboo sections of the interior plateau are prov- ince's main cattle-ranching areas. The Douglas Ranch near Kamloops and the Gang Ranch near Williams Lake are among the large-scale operations; the Gang Ranch is said to have the largest acreage of any ranch on the con-

Seine fishing is profitable in British Columbia waters.

WILLIAMS BROS.

tinent, but a considerable proportion of its area is mountainous and not highly productive.

Though only some 3 or 4 per cent of the province's land area is rated as agricultural land and only about one-sixth of this is now under cultivation, the annual farm cash income is about $120,000,000 a year. Soil experts point out that the Skeena and Bulkley River valleys have about 1,000,000 acres of good land as yet undeveloped and that the Peace River Block has at least 2,000,000. Farm experts are less enthusiastic, emphasizing difficulties of climate, transportation, and high cost of development. Still more good land could be developed by large irrigation projects that might be combined with flood control and the production of hydroelectric power. At present only about 25,000 acres of new land are being brought into production each year, and it would be wrong to suggest that any agricultural boom is in sight. But the province has room for agricultural settlers with capital, and there can be no doubt that undeveloped lands will one day be put to use.

The commercial fisheries of British Columbia include what is probably the greatest salmon river in the world—the Fraser. This great stream is open to the salmon from its mouth to its sources in the Rockies and the Omineca Mountains, far up in the heart of the province. It draws on an immense complex of lakes and tributary streams, nearly all of which have their specialized runs and races of salmon and some of which—Stuart, Quesnel, Chilco, and Adams, to name the most famous—provide ideal conditions for hatching and rearing the red or sockeye salmon, now probably the most valuable of the five Pacific species.

The Fraser has suffered greatly from mismanagement in the past. The rockslides at Hell's Gate Canyon in 1913, a useless gold-mining dam on the Quesnel River, and a small logging dam on the Adams River combined to reduce the runs and in some cases destroy them completely. But the work of the International Pacific Salmon Fisheries Commission, created by treaty between Canada and the United States, has done much to restore the runs to their former abundance. In 1958 the Adams River run brought back over 18,000,000 fish. The Quesnel River run has been increased from a few score of scattered spawners to more than 200,000—enough to produce a run of 10,000,000 or 12,000,000 adult fish under favorable conditions. There have been disappointments, mainly due to unknown conditions at sea: the Quesnel River run of 1961 was one of these and the Adams River run of 1962 has proved to be another. But these are temporary setbacks and there is good reason to believe that within the next twenty years the river will be regularly producing runs at least as great as—perhaps greater than—those of its natural abundance. Most of the returning salmon are caught as they

The rich harvest of the sea.

WILLIAMS BROS.

B. C. Hydro Building in Vancouver symbolizes the role of hydro power in the economic life of the province.   B. C. GOVERNMENT PHOTO

pass down the west coast of Vancouver Island and into the Strait of Juan de Fuca on their way to the river mouth. Fishing is regulated to provide equal catches for United States and Canadian fishermen.

While the Fraser is supreme, other great rivers of the province, such as the Nass and the Skeena, support major salmon runs, and about 1000 lesser streams contribute to the abundance that makes a great sports fishery as well as a great commercial industry. Herring, halibut, ground fish, crabs, clams, and other shellfish also contribute to the commercial catch, which supports some 12,000 fishermen operating more than 9000 boats. With shore workers in the canning and packing plants, supporting industries, and service industries, it is estimated that the province's fisheries employ about 90,000 people.

Since the war, British Columbia has begun to realize that she has immense sources of energy in the hydro power of her rivers and in the newly discovered gas and oil fields of the Peace River country. Some 40,000,000 horsepower of energy pours down the rivers each year, and at the present time less than 3,500,000 horsepower is harnessed. Natural-gas reserves of over 70,000,000,000,000 cubic feet have been indicated in the Peace River Block by wells drilled to date, and there is good reason to believe that these can be greatly increased by further drilling.

Development of the huge hydro potential presents many serious problems, some of them insuperable in the present state of knowledge and likely to remain so for a long while to come. Hydroelectric installations in the main channels of major salmon streams—such as the Fraser, Nass, and Skeena, for instance—are out of the question if the salmon runs are to be preserved. Smaller dams near the headwaters or on selected tributary streams can be safely built but would realize only a fraction of the potential. Most British Columbia rivers are also subject to extreme fluctuations of flow: spring and summer flows from melting snow and glaciers may be as much as 100 times as great as those of the winter freeze-up. This, taken with the rapid fall of the rivers from the mountains and the narrowness of the valleys available for water storage, means that the flow can be controlled and fully used only by very high and costly dams and diversion works.

So far, most developments have been on a fairly small scale, carefully planned to meet the needs of developing industry. But the largest single development, the Kemano plant built by the Aluminium Company of Canada for its works at Kitimat, is an exception. Here the Nechako River, one of the tributaries of the Fraser, was turned back on its course and tumbled abruptly down the steep western slope of the Coast Range to the head of Gardiner Canal, where it yields a potential of 1,800,000 horsepower, nearly

Columbia Lake, source of the Columbia River.   B. C. GOVERNMENT PHOTO

half of which is now in use. In this instance, a large user of electricity has chosen to bring its raw material to the power site and to manufacture there, even though the site is remote from ultimate markets. The brand-new municipality of Kitimat, incorporated in 1953, with a present population in excess of 10,000 is the result.

At the present time two very large projects are under active consideration. One, on the Upper Columbia River, is especially interesting in that it reflects complications produced by the historic decision that set the international boundary line along the forty-ninth parallel instead of by the natural run of the country, making the river international. Development on the American side has been very great, on the Canadian side almost negligible, to date. But it is obvious that any major Canadian development is bound to have a great effect on American works downstream.

After many years of hard work and even harder bargaining, an international joint commission developed a treaty that seemed acceptable to all the parties concerned—the U.S. government, the Canadian government, and the government of British Columbia. At last the great Columbia project seemed ready to go ahead. It would yield the United States full flood control on the river and greatly increased power capacity at the downstream dams. In return, British Columbia would receive half the increase in downstream power and a considerable cash payment for the flood-control benefits, while the works in Canada would make it possible to develop very cheaply all the hydro power needed in the province over the next ten years or more.

While all this was going on, Axel Wenner-Gren, the Swedish industrialist, was investigating the possibilities of developing a project of roughly equal size on the Peace River in northern British Columbia. It soon appeared that a great block of power could be developed on the Peace, though it was not likely to be competitive in price with the Columbia power and would probably have to wait until this was largely committed and a new demand developed.

This was the comparatively clear and simple picture only a year or so ago. Since that time, all has become chaos and confusion. Figures have been worked and reworked, twisted and shaded and distorted until nothing can be clear. The Wenner-Gren interests have withdrawn. The provincial government has stepped in by taking over the British Columbia Electric Company, the largest utility company in the province, and also the Wenner-Gren plans for the Peace River. As of this writing, the international treaty for the Columbia development has not been ratified by Canada and no one knows when or whether it will be. Most Canadians suspect that such a comedy of inept leadership and political scheming could be staged only in the delirious atmosphere of the Pacific province, and perhaps they are right. But the Columbia project makes too much sense to be lost in any political scramble. And there can be little doubt that it will go ahead in good order before very long, to the great benefit of the whole Northwest.

Energy in all its forms is going to play a large part in the future of British Columbia. It is readily available in the natural gas and oil of the Peace River Block, and the prospect of new discoveries there is very real. It is cheaply available in some of the province's coal reserves, such as the Hat Creek deposit near Lillooet. It is available on a number of rivers that do not

Empress Hotel and inner harbor of Victoria.   B. C. GOVERNMENT PHOTO

support major salmon runs. A good deal of the province's future prosperity must depend upon the skill and care with which all this energy is developed and used. While nuclear power should become economic in plenty of time to save the salmon streams, only a wise combination of the special advantages of energy from nuclear, natural-gas, coal, and hydro sources will ensure that an abundance of energy in its most desirable form will always be available for any development that may be proposed.

Parliament Buildings, Victoria.　　　　　　　　　B. C. GOVERNMENT PHOTO

Though natural resources are the base of British Columbia's economy, only 13 per cent of the labor force is employed in primary industry; a further 15 per cent is employed in the manufacturing industry, most of which is concerned with products of forests, fisheries, and farms; and no less than 72 per cent is employed in the service industries. This means that in spite of the province's vast size and small population, most British Columbians live urban lives; in other words, their habits and standards are much like those of the people of any other section of North America and include such features as commuting, annual vacations with pay, union mem-

English Gift Shop in Victoria.   B. C. GOVERNMENT PHOTO

bership, and a pension plan, together with such possessions as a suburban home, an automobile, a television set, and possibly a small cruiser or outboard boat, all at various stages of purchase. The visitor cannot really be sure of seeing an abundance of backwoodsmen and other unusual types or even of distinguishing them from ordinary citizens when seen; nor need he carry his own protective armament against wild animals, even though a cougar was shot in downtown Victoria only recently.

Vancouver and Victoria are the largest cities of the province and the most easily reached. Victoria has a special and delicate grace that is all

Victoria's residential districts take you back to England.   B. C. GOVERNMENT PHOTO

her own. Setting and climate favor her; history is on her side; Government House stands high on one of her hills; the Legislative Buildings and the Empress Hotel flank her inner harbor; and the Olympic Mountains shine in white splendor across the Straits of Juan de Fuca. Her pace is calm, unruffled by industrial excitements, yet not without cheerful echoes of a gaiety that has grown and persisted since colonial days. Her schools and newspapers are the best in the province; she is called old-fashioned and stubbornly British but is far too poised and confident to change her ways. The rest of the province may have its money, its newness, its hysterical

Vancouver is the financial, industrial, shipping, and cultural center of the province.
WILLIAMS BROS.

dedication to growth and progress, but, as James Douglas made plain long ago, the real decisions are made in Victoria.

Victoria is kind to visitors. She has her noble hotel and a few good restaurants, notably the Swiss Restaurant on Old Esquimalt Road; she has stores full of glass and china and woolens and antiques, excellent golf courses and beautiful flower gardens. Pupils of the late Chief Mungo Martin carve massive totem poles in the ancient tradition in Thunderbird Park. Beacon Hill Park, with its seascapes and skylarks, is a step away from downtown. There are summer symphonies in Butchart's Gardens out by

Granville Street—gay, neon-lit, and a bit tawdry—is the commercial heart of Vancouver.
WILLIAMS BROS.

Brentwood Bay and a small art gallery that offers many pleasant surprises. Over in the Parliament Buildings the Provincial Museum shows with dedicated care what little it can of a great collection of primitive Indian art in a sad little basement space; the Provincial Archives cherish the Province's history under almost equally inadequate conditions. A new building is said to be on the drawing boards and conceivably it may materialize while this book is still being read. But even in their present quarters, both the Museum and the Archives are well worth a visit.

Vancouver, by contrast with Victoria, is a big city and almost a brash one. It is incontestably the financial, industrial, shipping, and cultural center of the province, and it is also, in spite of the rawness and errors of rapid growth, a very nice place. It has extended to cover a great peninsula, with the estuary of the Fraser River on the south, the Gulf of Georgia to the west, and Burrard Inlet, its noble harbor, to the north. Across Burrard Inlet are the dormitory cities of North and West Vancouver, linked to the metropolis by the slender, graceful span of Lion's Gate Bridge, across the First Narrows of the inlet. High over these two cities, rising out of their back yards, are the North Shore Mountains.

Vancouver is one of the world's great ports and certain to become steadily greater as trade with the Orient increases. Years ago, in the days of the P. and O. liners and the graceful white ships of the Canadian Pacific fleet, it was one of the world's great crossroads. Today the Orient and Pacific Line again serves Australasia and the South Seas and ships of a score of national registries call regularly. From the city's International Airport planes leave westward for the Orient, southward for Australia, northward for Europe by way of the North Pole, and eastward for the rest of Canada. Most ambitious travelers will find themselves in Vancouver, however briefly, before they finally fold their wings and go to rest.

In spite of its size and vigor, Vancouver is not an intimidating city. The main stores and hotels, most of the big office buildings, the Public Library, the Art Gallery, and the Queen Elizabeth theater are all agreeably concentrated within a few blocks. Stanley Park, with its tall trees, its Theater under the Stars, and a small but interesting aquarium and zoo, is less than a mile from downtown. Beaches—periodically polluted, it is true—are everywhere. Salmon can be caught at most seasons within an hour or so of the city center. The University of British Columbia, huge, young, and growing much too fast, is within half an hour's drive of the Vancouver Hotel. Its campus at Point Grey, where George Vancouver met the Spaniards Galiano and Valdez in 1792, is one of the most beautiful in the world.

Each year, in July and August, Vancouver holds its International Festival of the Arts. The festival lasts several weeks and includes everything

Tall firs stand in cathedral-like aisles in Stanley Park, Vancouver.   WILLIAMS BROS.

Upper Levels highway winds tortuously above Gulf of Georgia along the North Shore Mountains.   B. C. GOVERNMENT PHOTO

from chamber music to full-dress opera, from a play to a monologue, from a film to a military tattoo by searchlight. Great performers come from all over the world and the city briefly denies the burden of its cautious Nordic origins and becomes truly *en fête*. Nothing better or more promising has ever happened to Vancouver or to British Columbia, and few provincial cities anywhere can offer the visitor a more ambitious or rewarding spell of entertainment.

Beyond these southern cities lies the British Columbia that gives them reason for being—the land of forests and mountains and water, of fish

Fort Steele—the white gleam of snow and glacier against blue sky.

and fertile fields and wild creatures. In spite of careless logging, mistreatment of watersheds, and development that makes no effort to hide its ugliness, it remains a great, wild land, full of beauties and wonders for anyone with eyes to see and a heart to feel.

Any land that is half mountains must, I suppose, be beautiful. Whatever the people of the plains may think, mountains make for views across distance, for incredible lights and shadows at sunrise and sunset, for a sense of mass and majesty and reach. The white gleam of snow and glacier against blue sky, the fall of cascading water over rock faces, the formidable

Blue skies and sharply etched green landscapes greet summer passengers on the Gulf Island ferries.   A. M. SHARP

shapes of peaks, and the immensity of slides and precipices touch most people and stir a sense of wonder in them that is healthy for the soul. Go where you will in British Columbia, you will find such things, and find them always in different form and scale and proportion.

Perhaps it is logical to think first of the East Kootenays and the Rocky Mountain Trench. Four national parks—Yoho, Glacier, Kootenay, and Mount Revelstoke—open up some of the finest scenery in the Rockies and the Selkirks. Here, too, are the sources of the Columbia; the Kootenay River, looping southward into Montana and Idaho and crossing the border north again to Kootenay Lake and its junction with the Columbia proper below the Arrow Lakes; and the Columbia itself, crossing the highway as a fair-sized creek and going on to build its strength from the two great mountain ranges as it makes the northward curve around the Selkirks by Kinsbasket Lake and David Thompson's Boat Encampment and Mica Creek to Revelstoke and its widening in the Arrow Lakes.

The Coast Range, comparable in size and grandeur to the Rockies themselves, starts by Vancouver, on the north shore; climbs at once to the meadows and peaks of Garibaldi Park; finds its greatest height in Mount Waddington, between Bute and Knight inlets; and holds on northward to the St. Elias Mountains in Alaska. It is rugged and difficult country, heavy with timber and brush on the western slopes, nursing its ice-age glaciers above timber line, in many places still untrodden even by the boots of the mountaineer. Yet great arms of the sea lead in among the feet of the mountains, accepting waterfalls straight from the glaciers and slides from the peaks, branching into narrow valleys with lively streams. The sheltered waters of the Inside Passage make Jervis, Toba, Bute, Loughborough, Knight, and others of the great inlets readily and safely accessible to the small-boat enthusiast. From the Island Highway along the east coast of Vancouver Island these great mountains may be seen again across the water; and Vancouver Island has her own high mountains as well, scarcely less formidable and no less beautiful.

The mountains are inevitable, and no visitor can escape them. They rear above the Fraser's canyons, fringe the interior plateau, crowd in again to the northward. But unless one is a dedicated mountaineer—and perhaps even then—they have their limits of value. Most of us want something a little more approachable and friendly. There is blossomtime in the Okanagan Valley, when whole hillsides light with the white and pink of the fruit blossoms above the lovely lakes. There are Penticton's August Peach Festival, with dancing in the streets, and Kelowna's International Regatta, which draws swimmers and divers and water skiers from all over the continent. There is the annual stampede at Williams Lake in the Cariboo, second in Canada only to Calgary's; there are loggers' sports at Sooke on Vancouver Island, a July First lamb barbecue on Saturna Island, Vernon's Winter Carnival at Silver Star, Indian Festivals at Victoria and Brentwood, salmon derbies, steelhead derbies, canoe races, bonspiels for curlers, Highland games for caber tossers, golf tournaments for the orthodox. From May to September in every year someone somewhere is putting on a show. And once every four years, in the cycle of 1962–1966–1970, the sockeye salmon put on the greatest show of all as they come home in their scarlet millions, by Hell's Gate on the Fraser, by the Thompson River to Shuswap Lake and the spawning grounds in Adams River—some 300 acres of what has been called "the richest gravel in the world." It is late in the season, an October show, but there is nothing else like it anywhere in the world—the greatest of salmon runs to the greatest of salmon rivers. Both white and Indian people of the Shuswap country honor it in a festival they call "Salute to the Sockeye."

Some people, no doubt, are enthusiasts for festivals and fairs and regattas, but most of us can take them as we find them or do without them unless we happen on them. Most people who come to British Columbia and get past the cities into the hinterland just want to wander around and look at this and that in peace; some 85 per cent of them, if statistics can be believed, also want to get in a little fishing, either on the side or as the main purpose of the trip. Wherever the balance lies, the combination of purposes is a good one, and British Columbia is a good place to realize it.

Fishing, of course, is a subject all of its own and deserves more serious consideration than a paragraph or two in a general discussion of the province. But a few useful generalizations are possible.

The best salmon fishing in the province is at the coast, mainly trolling in salt water. The best trout fishing in the province is in the lakes of the interior plateau, where the Kamloops variety of rainbow trout achieves miracles of growth and performance. Most of the salmon fishing is provided by two species, the spring or king salmon, which averages about twenty pounds and reaches weights of seventy pounds and over, and the coho or silver salmon, which averages from five to ten pounds through the season and occasionally weighs twenty pounds or more. A third species, the pink or humpback salmon, is also frequently taken by anglers. In addition to the salmon fishing, there is some good trout fishing in many of the coastal streams; the cutthroat trout are abundant in most coastal lakes. In the eastern part of the province both cutthroat and rainbow trout are often abundant. North of the Prince George-Prince Rupert Highway, on the Arctic watershed, there is good fishing for Arctic grayling, especially in the tributary streams that run down from the Omenica Mountains into the Parsnip. The best fishing for steelhead, the big sea-running rainbows, is wherever you find it, but nearly all the Vancouver Island streams have good winter runs and such streams as the Morice, Kispiox, Babine, and Sustut on the Skeena-Bulkley watershed have good fall runs.

In other words, there is fishing to be had almost anywhere in the province, subject always to the fisherman's usual disappointments through arriving too early or too late or in the wrong weather or with his rabbit's foot in the wrong pocket. The true enthusiast will inform himself on these matters and endeavor to keep them all in order. But the happier sportsman,

Salmon fishing at Alberni Canal on Vancouver Island.   RAY ATKESON

who takes his fishing as he finds it while looking over the country and enjoying other things, can pack his rods and gear with the assurance that wherever he goes, fishing of one sort or another will not be far away.

The favorite haunt of the salmon fisherman is along the shores of the Gulf of Georgia, either by way of Vancouver Island's east coast and the highway that runs from Victoria to Kelsey Bay or by the ferry and road links along the mainland coast from Howe Sound to Pender Harbor, Powell River, and Lund. On the Vancouver Island side, Cowichan Bay, Qualicum,

Comox, Oyster River, and Campbell River are favorite centers. Travel among these is easy, pleasant, and rewarding. There are provincial camp-sites in many beautiful places, such as Englishman's River Falls, Little Qualicum Falls, Miracle Beach, and Elk Falls. Hotels and motels are abundant. The east coast of the island is a lovely place to be at any time, and there are plenty of attractive side issues, such as good beaches, fine mountains, and good trout lakes and streams.

But Vancouver Island also has a west coast. It is largely inaccessible by road, but not entirely so. A good paved highway runs over the divide from Parksville to Alberni and continues on to Sproat Lake. From there, is a logging road, open to the public from 5 P.M. to 7 A.M. and on weekends. It is rough and bumpy and dusty, but beautiful, by Sproat Lake and Taylor River and Kennedy River to Kennedy Lake and the twenty-four miles of public road between Ucluelet and Tofino. Here is the open Pacific, rolling, changing, magnificent, with its beaches and points and bays and rocky islets. Here is the tremendous sandy sweep of Long Beach—which is properly Wickaninnish Bay, in honor of the great Nootka war chief of the nineteenth century. Here are Wreck Bay and Schooner Bay and Quisitis Point, with their thundering surf and sea palms and sea anemones and starfish and oyster catchers; here is Ucluelet, with its great fleet of commercial trolling vessels; here is Tofino, with the sheltered waters behind it and the great mud flats that make the finest resting place on the Pacific Flyway for ducks and wild geese. If I were a visitor to Vancouver Island with only a casual thought of salmon in the back of my mind, I should want to make this trip above all and take my chances on the salmon.

It is not so very different in the interior. If you are a dyed-in-the-wool fisherman, you probably have your lake in mind and know its times and moods, at least by hearsay—Paul or Stump or Taweel, LeJeune or Pennask, or wherever it is. But what of the Lillooet Mountains and some of the secrets they hold? What about a pack trip to the Elk and the Wigwam rivers over by Fernie in the East Kootenays? What about risking the rough gravel of the Chilcotin Road toward Bella Coola, where the sweeping, grassy hills climb up to the timber line among the clumps of creeping juniper? There are fish to be had up that way, in Nimpo Lake and the Dean River and the Bella Coola River. No country is lovelier, and it is the country of the Chilcotin War, where the shades of Chiefs Alexis and Klattasine, Tellot, Pielle, and the others still roam the hills they knew so well that $80,000 and a punitive expedition led by the best white woodsmen in the country could not come up with them.

Farther north, at Quesnel, it is an easy drive into Barkerville, the ghost

Church at Barkerville, a ghost town of gold-rush days.   B. C. GOVERNMENT PHOTO

Prince George, some 500 miles by road from Vancouver, seems like the north itself but it is still only halfway up the province. B. C. GOVERNMENT PHOTO

town of the gold rush, which is now preserved as a Provincial Park. Across the Fraser, over more bad roads, is Alexander Mackenzie's West Road River, which is a fine rainbow-trout stream in its better moments.

Beyond Prince George it is an easy drive to Fort McLeod, the first white settlement in British Columbia, and only a little way on from there to the bridge across the Parsnip River, with Arctic grayling and Rocky Mountain whitefish and Dolly Varden char waiting for the fly above and below it. Just beyond Fort Fraser, on the road to Prince Rupert, is the Stellaco River, with its big surface-feeding rainbows. Beyond there is the Morice, with its September coho salmon and steelhead; the Fulton, with its Millionaire's Pool and rainbow-crowded riffles—but why go on? It is all holiday country, the kind North Americans look for and understand, with things to see and do, places to camp, motels for a shower and a dry bed, fish to be fished for and even caught.

For the big-game hunter, whether he uses rifle or camera or just a pair of binoculars, the province also has much. Grizzly and black bears; elk; moose; mountain goats; sheep of several species; woodland caribou; blacktail, mule, and whitetail deer—all are abundant in their particular ranges. In the mountains of the East Kootenays, near Fernie, is some of the most accessible and least exploited big-game country left on the continent, where record trophies are still a possibility. If you have the time and money, the chance is even better in the Cassiar Mountains of the north, an unspoiled wilderness of splendid horse country, unfished lakes, and game-producing hills.

The upland bird hunter will find blue grouse on the hills, pheasants in the Okanagan Valley, chukar partridge on the sagebrush slopes of the Thompson Valley, prairie chicken and ruffed grouse in the Peace River Block. The bird lover who does not shoot can surprise and delight himself a thousand times in a thousand places throughout his unlimited seasons with shore birds and songbirds, swans and pelicans, sand-hill cranes and long-billed curlews. In spring and summer the Cariboo parklands seem to welcome everything that flies.

I have been accused of carrying on a drawn-out love affair with British Columbia, mostly in print and in public. It may be so. Propinquity counts for much in such affairs. In British Columbia I live and work and have my being. But I am a critical and often irritable lover. Nothing here has the shiny and sterile perfection the travel folders show. It is a splendid country, exciting in a hundred different ways. But you will not find it without looking. You will not enjoy it to the full without searching and understanding. You will not travel through it without discomfort or reach its finest moments without a little effort. Nor can you hope to see more than a little part of it in a summer, a year, or a lifetime.

British Columbia, in its strange and manifold ways, is a whole, an entity. It is a way of thinking and being. It is Canadian, but it is also West Coast Canadian, never quite forgetful of the mountains that divide and frustrate while they make the climate and lakes and rivers and forests and fisheries and mines. It is a boastful, flamboyant, extroverted sort of a place, only

Mile O on the Alaska Highway is where the north really begins.

B. C. GOVERNMENT PHOTO

The Inside Passage between Vancouver Island and the mainland. WILLIAMS BROS.

now beginning to ask questions about itself, to wonder where it came from and where it is going. Though the traveler may see only one small corner of the province, he will, if he is aware, sense something of this. Having sensed it, he will be able to measure the rest against it and know that, in spite of surfaced highways and gimcrack towns with jukeboxes in the restaurants, he is in a country that is still pioneering its way into a future.

Index